NAUGHTY
Girl's GUIDE TO
LAS VEGAS

Naughty Girl's Guide to Las Vegas
www.NaughtyTravelGuide.com

Published by Naughty Girl Press
1158 26th St. Suite 207
Santa Monica, CA 90403
www.NaughtyGirlPress.com

First Edition 2014

ISBN: 978-0-9852123-2-2

Every effort was made to make sure that this book is up-to-date as much as
possible at the time of going to print. Some details such as websites, telephone
numbers and addresses are likely to change. And some places may even go out
of business by the time you read this book. My advice would be to call or visit
the businesses' websites before visiting. The author and publisher of *Naughty
Girl's Guide to Las Vegas* cannot accept responsibility for facts that have become
outdated or situations that arise from the use of this book.

NAUGHTY Girl's GUIDE TO LAS VEGAS

Sienna Sinclaire

Dedicated to my two naughty travel companions. Thanks for helping me research the book and taking a few for the team.

Contents

WHO IS THE NAUGHTY VEGAS GIRL?

When you visit Las Vegas you can't help but want to be naughty because it's everywhere. Even if you're normally not a naughty girl, Vegas will always bring it out of you when you least expect it. And I'm here, as your naughty tour guide, to show you how—as we all have an inner "Naughty Girl" in all of us.

As a tourist or a local, you may think that Las Vegas is for men because of all the eye candy and advertisements geared toward them, such as strip clubs and escorts, but it's actually a woman's city. Women are what make Vegas what it is. They may have tons of strip clubs, but we can enjoy them just as much as men and there are some that offer male strippers. There are sexy Vegas shows that feature scantily clad women on stage, but there are shows with half-naked men in them, too. There may be tons of strippers and escorts for men to pay to talk to them, but us women get free male attention and they even buy us drinks!

We get many things for free in Vegas that men don't. Besides the free attention from the opposite (and sometimes the same!) sex, we get free entry into clubs—and some of them even offer free drinks for women before a certain time. There are private swingers' parties that men can't get into unless they are with a woman, whereas women can get in by themselves or with as many girlfriends as they want. You can be just as naughty as a guy if you wish. Why let the guys engage in all the debauchery?

I'm going to show you the best places to see live male strip shows, the best places for a sexy rendezvous with your lover or a stranger, and more—so you can be as naughty as you want. What happens in Vegas doesn't really count anyway, because you're supposed to let your hair down. It's okay to act a little wild, drink more than usual, wear scantily clad dresses, have sex with a stranger or even pay for sex. It's Vegas, where naughtiness isn't just accepted, it's a way of life.

xoxo Sienna Sinclaire

Naughty History

LAS VEGAS' NAUGHTY HISTORY

How did a dusty little railroad town in the Nevada desert turn into one of the naughtiest cities in the world? It tapped into something other American cities couldn't or wouldn't promote: vices.

There's no hiding from sex in this city. It is everywhere you look—from giant billboards promoting topless shows to flyers for escort services handed out on every block of the Strip. Where else in the world can you find almost every vice openly encouraged?

Vegas is the adult playground and strip club capital of the world. The city's motto of "What happens in Vegas, stays in Vegas" holds true as long as you don't post your naughtiness all over your social networks. But if you're like me, you don't mind showing the world how naughty you are!

The one constant for Las Vegas—which started in the early 1900s with the completion of the railroad—is the lure of sex. Vegas quickly became known for the infamous Block 16, where railway passengers could drink, gamble, and hire prostitutes.

THE BEGINNING OF LAS VEGAS

Las Vegas started as a railroad hub and stop-off point between Salt Lake City and Los Angeles. Its location between the two cities and its proximity to two large, freshwater springs made it an ideal spot for the railroads' repair shops. William Clark, aspiring railroad tycoon and U.S. senator from Montana, saw the area as a perfect spot to connect the two burgeoning cities and to make a killing in real estate.

The first lots in town cost between $150 to $750. This was expensive for the early 1900s, so Clark needed a way to convince potential buyers to come to the middle of the desert and set up shop here. He took out newspaper ads on both coasts that promised to refund train fare to anyone who bought one of his lots.

Sensing a good thing, a year earlier in 1904, a railroad surveyor named J.T. McWilliams had begun selling lots (for even cheaper rates) on an eighty-acre parcel west of the tracks. By January 1905, McWilliams' site was already full of shopkeepers and merchants hoping to cash in on the new settlers. And demand for lots on Clark's site was so heavy that he had to sell most at auction on May 15, 1905. During the auction, the railroad company stipulated that no liquor could be sold on any of the premises, except for those in Block 17 and the infamous Block 16.

However, it wasn't all success for McWilliams and Clark. Many people just up and left their lots without ever opening their doors, and other arrivals took one look at the Las Vegas landscape and took the next train out. Then a huge fire on June 6, 1905 destroyed most of McWilliams' site. The town was in an economic death spiral, so the city's founders looked to the main thing bringing in revenue: vice.

There were many non-naughty businesses in Las Vegas at the time, but Block 16 was becoming the biggest moneymaker. Cowboys, prospectors, drifters, curiosity seekers, and rail passengers all came to drink, gamble, and screw.

BLOCK 16: THE RED LIGHT DISTRICT

The best way to describe Block 16 is to imagine dusty saloons full of "gambling tables, whiskey, and gin flowing like a river, and scantily clad women with loose morals"[1] waving out of every window. It's where Las Vegas got the name "Sin City." And at the time, it was the only form of entertainment in town.

It's no longer there, but you can still visit its location on First Street between Ogden and Stewart Avenues (two blocks from Fremont Street and one block from Main Street). Block 16 got its name from the original town map of the city, and it became famous in 1906 by unapologetically offering prostitution. At first, both Blocks 16 and 17 had become increasingly popular for being the only two blocks that could serve alcohol legally, but Block 16 eventually differentiated itself from Block 17 by moving more towards prostitution.

Block 16 was also the only place in the city where women could work, so that pretty much left prostitution the only job available. Most prostitutes would rent rooms in the back or upper floors of the saloons to entertain their clients. The women paid part of their profits to the owner. While the customers got loose with their morals, and, more importantly, their cash, most of the girls drank colored water. Someone had to be the sober one, after all. Also, the girls had to go to a doctor once a week for examinations as a sick girl couldn't work.

Block 16 was not only famous for its ladies of the night, but also for selling booze during the Prohibition Era. As a result, Block 16 was legendary all the way to Washington and was the target of many raids. However, they continued to sell alcohol all the way through Prohibition.

BUILDING OF THE HOOVER DAM

Paradoxically, even though Las Vegas was notorious for alcohol sales and consumption, the Prohibition laws were increasingly putting a wet blanket on the party. By 1928 Vegas was barely surviving—mostly due to fears of a government crackdown on establishments and customers. The state tried a couple of things to lure people to visit or move there over the next few years. It shortened the residency requirement for divorce and legalized gambling in 1931, and it banned sales, income, inheritance, and corporate taxes in the hopes of attracting big business.

Additionally, President Calvin Coolidge gave the city a big break when he signed a bill for the construction of the Boulder Dam (later named the Hoover Dam). The city even played nice for a few days in 1929 when President Hoover sent his new Secretary of the Interior, Lyman Wilbur, to visit the dam site and the town. All saloons, gambling clubs, and brothels closed their doors during his visit. Their little trick may have worked if some local newspaper reporters hadn't taken a member of the Wilbur party on a "behind-the-scenes" naughty tour of Vegas.

After this was discovered, the government decided it would be in the best interests of the dam workers to keep them away from so much vice. They declared the site a federal reservation, which made it illegal (under federal law, at least) for a single man to gamble, drink, or have sex with a woman there.

The workers didn't mind because Las Vegas was only ten miles away, therefore, business on Block 16 boomed. It was a high time for the city, but Las Vegas was now facing another potential economic downturn with the completion of the Hoover Dam, as workers were leaving. Vegas needed another hook to make money off its naughty girl ways.

QUICKIE DIVORCES

In 1931 Nevada shrunk the three-month residency requirement for a divorce to just six weeks (instead of the year it would take in most states along with proof of adultery in some cases). If you had the money, you could take an extended month and a half vacation by staying in a hotel, boarding house, or a "divorce ranch" and then see a judge for a quick hearing.

Vegas cashed in on the notoriety made in 1939 when Ria Langham Gable came to town to divorce her movie star husband, Clark Gable. The city and the local papers kept the story quiet for the six-week waiting period, as agreed upon by Mrs. Gable and her lawyer. With her agreement of keeping her divorce quiet, Mrs. Gable posed for photos showing her living it up in the city for the papers to use after her divorce for publicity.

The plan worked. After Ria's divorce, Las Vegas became the place to get divorced in 1939. The city could barely keep up with the demand as people came from all over the state and country (and especially from L.A.) to dump their spouse. Smart entrepreneurs created "divorce ranches" for the wealthy to wait out their six weeks. Some of these ranches, like the

Boulderado Ranch and Tule Springs, are now on the National Register of Historic Places.

HELLDORADO DAYS

Always on the lookout for an angle, local business owners searched for ways to make Las Vegas a permanent tourist destination. They decided to combine the town's reputation for depravity with Americans' love of nostalgia and began promoting their sleepy desert outpost as the one and only place in the country where Americans could still experience the Old West.

Las Vegas' Helldorado Days began in 1934 when Arizona carnival barker Clyde Zerby saw a way to make money off workers at the Hoover Dam site and the thousands of visitors who flocked to see it being built.

"The first Helldorado was a rowdy affair, featuring a 'hoochie coochie dance' show and other attractions that would let dam workers blow-off steam."[2] Las Vegas was a booming town in 1935, but city leaders knew the boom could end at any time and Las Vegas could wind up a ghost town once construction of Hoover Dam was complete.

Local Elks Lodge No. 1468 created the annual Helldorado Days festival. It was promoted as a way for locals and tourists to experience the Old

West. It was wildly popular, however, in order to build a community and get families to come out, the naughtier activities were taken out.

In the end it was not the Helldorado Days that would turn Las Vegas into the place to go for fun. It was its close proximity to Los Angeles and its talent for making the most of its naughty ways. What other city allowed prostitution, gambling, quickie divorces, and the "pursue your desires and we won't ask a lot of questions" attitude all in one town? Before long, you could even find every desire on just one street.

THE BEGINNING OF THE STRIP

Tom Hull, a Los Angeles hotel magnate, knew that trains were quickly fading in popularity and that cars would soon be the way people traveled the country. So, he built the El Rancho casino on some cheap land three miles from downtown Las Vegas and opened it on April 3, 1941.

At first everyone thought he was crazy, but they soon realized he was a genius as his hotel set the stage for future resorts that would become The Strip. Plus he offered a chorus line of nearly naked women, The El Rancho Girls, that performed at his showroom called the Opera House. Soon, every hotel in Vegas had exotic dancers. That led to the casinos bringing in bigger and bigger stars in attempts to outdo each other.

But it wasn't all success for Tom Hull. The one failure that got the most attention was in 1958 when he opened a new show featuring women wearing only hats and shoes. Yes, the show was hugely successful with customers. However, other goody-goody locals caused an uproar and soon Hull had to eliminate all nudity from his shows.

In 1942, theater mogul R.E. Griffith and his nephew, architect William J. Moore, opened a new hotel down the road called Hotel Last Frontier. It was renamed the New Frontier in 1955, following a modernization of the resort. One of the bars at the Last Frontier, was called the Gay Nineties. It featured many famous burlesque dancers of the time.

Another popular venue that opened, featuring a sexy dance troupe called the Flora-Dora Girls, was the Golden Slipper Saloon and Gambling Hall (later renamed the Silver Slipper). It opened in 1950 as part of the Last Frontier Village and it hosted popular entertainment and burlesque shows from 1950 thru 1988. It was wildly popular due to featuring famous burlesque performers such as Sally Rand, and shows like Barry Ashton's "Wonderful World of Burlesque." Ashton's shows featured dancers, strippers, comics, and nude showgirls.

However, the Silver Slipper wouldn't shine on forever. Billionaire Howard Hughes purchased it on April 30, 1968. It's said that he bought the place because the lights from the rotating slipper bothered him when he was in his hotel room across the street at the Desert Inn. He feared for his safety at this time and was known to be a little crazy. So after trying many times to get them to turn off the slipper, he decided he had had enough. He bought the casino and then had the slipper taken down.

THE END OF THE BROTHELS

Block 16 was eventually forced to close its brothels in 1942. A lot of local residents made efforts to keep Block 16 open for business, but they failed. Another effort to bring Block 16 back to life happened after WWII, but most of the buildings had been condemned by the city.

Brothels were almost legalized across the state in 1949. However, Governor Vail Pittman vetoed these efforts after strong pressure from the hotel-casino owners, who didn't want tourists to leave the city limits. Even though Block 16 was closed, this didn't end prostitution in Vegas. Many brothel owners just moved to other areas of the city, such as the "Four Mile."

"Four Mile" was the nickname of a community called Formyle. It was in the same valley as Las Vegas and had a natural spring. One popular establishment there was Roxie's. It was owned and operated by Eddie Clippinger, a one-time Los Angeles policeman, and his wife Roxie. Their business, which included a motel and nightclub, was highly successful, earning an estimated $1 million a year.

Other brothels included The Kassabian Ranch and C-Bar-C, which were located in Paradise Valley, a little off the Strip. The Kassabian was shut-down by the county vice squad in 1946 and the C-Bar-C burned to the ground in a possible arson.

Roxie's was able to stay open because it had the secret support of Sheriff Glen Jones. However, that all came to an end in 1954 when the FBI raided Roxie's. The G-men charged the Clippingers under the Mann act, which made it illegal to transport women across state lines for immoral pur-poses. That put an end to prostitution in Las Vegas, but brothels were allowed outside of Vegas in certain counties.

Joe Conforte, owner of the Mustang Ranch, convinced the county to pass an ordinance in 1971 that licensed brothels and kept them from being closed as a public nuisance.

Meanwhile, Roy Woofter, a friend of Conforte, was elected district attorney of Clark County. Woofter introduced an ordinance (although at one point he claimed it had been proposed by someone else) allow-ing one brothel to operate in Las Vegas in a high-walled security com-pound off Interstate 15 and pay $100,000 a year in fees. He gathered a good amount of local support, including some county commissioners (three of whom claimed legal brothels would cut down on rapes, bur-glaries, and outbreaks of venereal diseases). But the hotel owners and convention bureau officials threw a fit as they wanted prostitution to be available (to bring in tourists), but not advertised and promoted (to keep down competition for tourist dollars).

State legislators passed Statute 244-345 {8} in 1971, rendering prostitution illegal in counties with a population of more than 250,000. This only applied to Clark County back then, and it essentially ended the local brothel movement. Conforte's Mustang Range closed within a year.

THE EMERGENCE OF BURLESQUE

Burlesque dancers provided naughty entertainment long before pole dancers and two-girl shower shows. Burlesque eventually became mainstream entertainment, but for many years it was a big part of what made Vegas, Vegas.

Harold Minsky and the Minsky family became synonymous with burlesque in the first decades of the twentieth century in New York City. The new owner of the Dunes Hotel, Major Riddle, wanted to bring the Minsky Follies to his hotel. So Minsky brought his lavishly produced "Follies" show to Las Vegas for a six-year run at the Dunes beginning in 1956.

After the "Follies" success, Riddle thought of bringing over a big, expensive production from Paris, but wanted to test the waters before investing. So, he hired Fredric Apcar to help produce "Vive Le Girls!"

"Vive Le Girls!" became one of the longest running shows on the Strip and was so successful that Riddle approached Apcar about his vision for a French spectacular. Apcar suggested that the famed "Casino de Paris" be brought over from Paris, and Riddle announced the new show in 1963.

It was scheduled to open during a quiet time in Vegas on December 23rd. Many hotels shut down their showrooms during the month of December because tourism dropped drastically. But somehow, Riddle and Apcar's holiday opening was a bit of marketing genius that brought in people during an otherwise slow time.

FAMOUS BURLESQUE DANCERS OF SIN CITY

Many legendary burlesque performers graced Las Vegas stages during the heydays of bump and grind. Lily St. Cyr, Evelyn West, Blaze Star, Candy Barr, Jennie Lee, Lilly Christine, Tura Satana, Dusty Summers ("Las Vegas' Only Nude Magician"), Irma the Body, Tempest Storm (who, it is said, had affairs with the likes of Elvis Presley and JFK), Sally Rand, and many more are enshrined in the city's Burlesque Hall of Fame.

Lily St. Cyr's infamous bubble bath and "reverse strip" (where she'd actually get dressed on stage) dances started in Las Vegas, and Sally

Rand's highly sexualized version of burlesque made an impact on the Las Vegas Strip and continues even today. Rand performed at the Last Frontier Hotel from May 1954 to January 1955—and she was 51 years old at the time!

Today burlesque has made a comeback in Las Vegas, with individual burlesque performers who appear around the city (which you can learn more about in the burlesque section of this book).

Dita Von Teese was performing at MGM Grand's Crazy Horse Paris until the show closed. Now Vegas has a new burlesque show in town called "Pinup" at the Stratosphere. The show is guaranteed to take you back in time to the glamour and glitz of old Las Vegas.

If you want to learn about the history of burlesque, then visit the Burlesque Hall of Fame or attend the Burlesque Hall of Fame Weekend, hosted once a year in Vegas. The Burlesque Hall of Fame is on Fremont Street in downtown Las Vegas. It's a small place, but adorable and full of vintage photos and showgirl props. Their Hall of Fame Weekend is a massive event that has workshops, costume designers, comedians, magicians, and, of course, many stunning performances by dancers from around the world. They even have a burlesque parade of the performers down Fremont Street. It's a must-see event.

SHOWGIRLS GO TOPLESS

The first classic Las Vegas showgirls, clad in big headdresses and rhinestone-covered bikinis, appeared in 1952 with Danny Thomas at the Sands Casino. They were an immediate sensation and became the symbol of the city.

Once the showgirls appeared at the Sands Casino, other casinos began a fierce competition to top each other by making their shows as lavish and memorable as possible. This spawned the showgirl fashion we know today: enormous headdresses and exquisite costumes. Famed producer Harold Minsky's "Follies" showgirls appeared on stage topless for the first time at the Desert Inn in 1957. Donn Arden's "Lido de Paris" followed by incorporating topless showgirls into a large stage production at the Stardust. It was wildly successful, running for 31 years.

"Lido de Paris" was obviously not the first nor the last French show in Las Vegas. Minsky, Lou Walter, and endless other, smaller operators had for years been producing "French" revues, but the "Lido de Paris" was a genuine French spectacle. Other hotels were quick to find their own authentic French Shows. Producer Matt Gregory brought "Nouvelle Eve" to the El Rancho in 1959; the Tropicana hired Lou Walter as entertainment producer, and he immediately flew to Paris to sign the "Folies-Bergère," which opened at the Tropicana in 1959; and

Frederick Apcar's even racier "Casino de Paris" began a long run at the Dunes in 1963.

Of course, these elaborate shows became even more expensive once the Vegas economy turned sour in the 1980s. The town was, for the first time in a long time, struggling to make money and decided to make Las Vegas a place for the whole family. As a result, many of the topless shows gave way to the acrobatic shows, comedians, and magic acts that are still popular today. And Jubilee, which features topless dancers, decided to add a family friendly version of their show in 1981.

Sadly, on March 28, 2009, right before their 50th anniversary, the Folies-Bergère at the Tropicana had their final performance. Currently, Jubilee is the only major production still featuring showgirls in all their glory. If you want to see a family friendly version of showgirls, then visit "Vegas! The Show," which pays homage to all of the great performers of the city's past. That includes, thankfully, the impact showgirls made not only on the town, but also on culture worldwide.

MOULIN ROUGE: THE HOTSPOT THAT BROKE ALL THE RULES

Josephine "the Creole Goddess" Baker was such a powerful force in 1950s Las Vegas that part of her contract stated that African-Americans could purchase tickets to her performances. The El Rancho tested her once, and she refused to perform.

When the Moulin Rouge opened in 1955, it was an immediate game-changer. Your skin color didn't matter at "The Rouge," as the locals called it. Located in West Las Vegas, where the African-American population lived, it was called "America's first interracial hotel" and gave hundreds of black people well-paying jobs.

Many famous black and white entertainers visited and performed there, including Lena Horne, Judy Garland, Marlene Dietrich, Nat King Cole, Sammy Davis Jr., Louis Armstrong, and Frank Sinatra. The Rouge even had their own line of sexy showgirls. They were featured on the June 20, 1955 cover of Life magazine.

The Rouge was the late-night after-hours party in Vegas at the time. After all the shows on the Strip would close, everyone would head to The Rouge around 3 a.m., including celebrities and Vegas headliners, to party till the sun came up. And it wasn't unlikely to have Frank Sinatra and/or Sammy Davis Jr. come in and start singing while everyone danced, gambled, and drank.

But the party wouldn't last long. The Rouge, sadly, closed six months after it opened due to bankruptcy. The building sat for decades and suffered a few fires, before finally being demolished in 2010.

STRIP CLUBS COME TO VEGAS

Most strip clubs in Vegas didn't start looking classy until the 1970s, but they were still bringing in high rollers with wads of cash looking for naughty entertainment. Entrepreneurs saw that people were willing to spend money even in the "low-end" clubs, so they figured an upscale, luxurious club would bring in more revenue.

Paul Perry, a former casino dealer, opened The Gay 90's and then the Palomino Club down the street in 1969. The Palomino Club became world famous. It wasn't like other strip clubs in the U.S. He made sure it had state-of-the-art sound systems, fancy seating, and plush bars. Even though the Palomino was obviously Perry's money maker, he kept the Gay 90's club, but it eventually became the Satin Saddle Topless club.

Perry's clubs were known for having some of the hottest dancers in town. Strippers as we call them today were much different back then, as they went on stage in elaborate costumes and put on twenty-minute shows. The Palomino Club even had a "Nightly Amateur Nude Dance Contest" that brought in amateurs and the occasional stripper auditioning for a job. It was even featured in Playboy in 1979.

Sometimes they were girls new in town and down on their luck, so it was a way for them to get some quick money. Other times a great-looking girl from the audience would get up on stage, dared by a friend, and the place would go wild. Perry paid all of them something, even if they didn't win. It went on nightly, so Perry sometimes had a difficult time finding authentic amateurs. He soon realized the audience mostly changed every night, so he would get the Go-Go dancers from upstairs to enter the amateur contest downstairs.

The Palomino Club has always been the only club in town with a full bar and fully nude dancers, thanks to the liquor license procured in the 1960s letting it be "grandfathered" into the modern era (with its license expiring in 2019). No one will say how it was allowed that perk, but one theory is that Paul Perry was a generous friend to the right political campaigns.

Paul Perry, believe it or not, wasn't keen on table or lap dancing when it first appeared in the '80s. He soon figured out there was more money to be made, so he added private rooms and poles to his club.

Strip clubs haven't changed much since then. There are just more options now (with over forty strip clubs in the city limits alone), but all the decadent basics are still there. You won't find strip clubs in casinos yet, even though they allow topless shows and have topless pools, but hopefully one day they will since casinos really are a one-stop place.

TOPLESS POOLS COME TO TOWN

Clark County laws permit a resort/hotel to provide an area where topless sunbathing is permitted, but it must be separated from all other swimming pool and guest areas, obstructed from the view of patrons in those areas, off-limits to all minors, and cannot be used for any special events, contests, or parties while any topless sunbathing is taking place. Additionally, if gaming is permitted in the topless pool area, it must be open to the public, and not just to hotel guests.

Vegas casinos already had topless shows, so the next logical step was to add topless pools to their list of attractions. Many tourists were from Europe, where women bathing topless was (and still is in many countries) not a big deal, so why not cater to these tourists by offering them (and curiosity seekers) the option?

Caesar's Palace was the first casino to open a topless pool in 1998. While the pool was initially marketed to European clients, the concept took off and became a bandwagon jumped on by other casinos once they saw the revenue brought in by having topless women poolside.

In 2008, the Rio Hotel and Casino was the first to take the topless pool to the next level by partnering with Sapphires Gentlemen's club to open its own topless pool, complete with exotic dancers. The Nevada Gaming Control Board wasn't thrilled with the idea, as the perception that such a place would bring a lot of (or rather, more) crime into the casino.

In a good-faith effort in late July 2009, the Rio hotel asked the Las Vegas Metropolitan Police Department to do an undercover investigation of the Sapphire Pool. However, it resulted in eleven arrests and the pool was immediately closed. It has since re-opened as the Voodoo Lounge and the Voo European Style (topless) pool. Sapphires eventually opened their own sexy pool with the dancers wearing pasties.

Topless pools may be fading, as the mix of topless women and pool areas filled with drunken patrons often makes them more trouble than they're worth to many casinos. There are still tons of "toptional" pools in Las Vegas, so you can still tan your boobies if you know where to go. You can learn where in my section on topless pools.

PORN COMES TO VEGAS

The Adult Entertainment Expo and the Adult Video News Awards (commonly known as the "AVN's") have been held in Las Vegas since 1985, with the first event being held at the Aladdin with over 600 guests. Then they moved to the Tropicana hotel where they had over 1,000 guests. And in 2006, the AVN Awards were held in the Venetian hotel and even broadcast on cable TV. With the bad economy, the AVN Awards were downsized and moved to the Hard Rock Hotel in 2012.

Los Angeles is still the epicenter of the adult industry, but there's plenty of porn shot in Vegas. Maybe one day the porn industry may move to Vegas. Sex sells, especially in Sin City, and it seems like it's only a matter of time before adult film companies move to the desert to share their sexy wares.

VEGAS CLEANS UP ITS ACT

"The 1990s began with a blare of trumpets heralding the rise of a turreted medieval castle, fronted by a moated drawbridge and staffed by jousting knights and fair damsels. Excalibur reflected the '90s marketing trend to promote Las Vegas as a family-vacation destination."[3] "Family Entertainment" was the new slogan on the strip.

Circus Circus had been a Vegas institution since the 1970s, but it opened an indoor theme park in 1993 to attract more families. The Luxor, Treasure Island, and MGM Grand soon followed suit when they all opened in 1993. The city leaders and hotel owners wanted a new look to the city and a new atmosphere to go with it. They were also worried about the millions of dollars they were losing thanks to decreased travel and tighter budgets caused by the weak 1990s economy.

So, the hotel owners went big. They spent billions on new hotels or remodeling efforts on iconic ones. The new places were massive structures that had to be seen to be believed and full of everything a family could want— roller coasters, shopping malls, kid-friendly stores, water parks, and more.

The plan worked. Commercials proudly proclaimed Las Vegas to be a family destination and families came in droves. It worked too well, however. The casinos' gambling revenue began to drop as parents, unable to take their kids onto the gambling floors with them, went to mini-golf courses or spent their time at the pool with the kids instead of heading to the blackjack tables or rows of slot machines. Many hotels noticed kids being left alone in rooms while the parents were gambling, which could cause lawsuits. So, many casinos cut out the amusement parks and kid-friendly atmosphere in less than a year's time. MGM Grand closed down their children's amusement park after just nine months and spending over $100 million to build it.

Vegas reinvented itself again in the late 1990s as a luxury destination with several new hotels eclipsing any that had come before. Steve Wynn's Bellagio (opened October 1998) and Mandalay Bay (opened March 1999) brought a European feel to both ends of the Strip, and the Venetian and Paris soon followed, both opening up in 1999. The Cosmopolitan, one of the newest hotel casinos on the Strip, promotes itself as a chic resort for sexy people. Luxury is back, seemingly to stay, in Sin City.

SIN CITY RETURNS TO ITS NAUGHTY ROOTS

Las Vegas spent the first half of the 1990s trying to promote a more wholesome look but it quickly gave up and returned to its naughty roots. The family friendly atmosphere didn't work because it wasn't as profitable as casino owners wanted.

So, Las Vegas is returning to what it does best: adult entertainment. More sex clubs are in town than ever before, and the number of strippers performing in town every night is staggering. Hotels that were once family friendly are now getting back in touch with their customers by offering topless pools, topless shows, sexy waitresses, and more. New hotels like Encore are adult party places that are built around nightclubs and sexy day clubs rather than kid-friendly activities. Even city officials, like Major Oscar Goodman, promote Vegas as a naughty town by saying, "We want it to be an adult playland. We want people to feel free. We want them to think that this is the place that they can come to and not have any inhibitions."

Mirage spokesman Alan Feldman said in 1993 when Vegas was trying to become more family friendly, "Vegas is an adult destination. It has been for the better part of sixty years and will be an adult destination for as long as any of us can see into the future."

NAUGHTY WOMEN OF VEGAS

Vegas wouldn't be the city it is today without women. Many people say it's a man's town, but it's really all about women. Yes, a man founded Las Vegas, but it was a woman, Helen Stewart, from whom he bought the land that became Las Vegas' town site. Yes, rail workers came to Vegas, but the brothels kept them here. Sex saved Las Vegas and has made it so popular today.

Ria Langham, better known as Mrs. Clark Gable, put Vegas on the cultural map with her famous divorce. Gambling may have brought people here, but lots of cities had gambling. But they didn't have the sexy showgirls, burlesque performers, or topless shows found in the Vegas casinos.

Sexy women are everywhere in Vegas and they are what keeps the men coming to town. Take out the sexy women, bartenders, waitresses, go-go dancers, strippers, working girls, and topless shows and you'll lose the (straight) men.

Sure, men come here to be naughty, but Vegas is also a big playground for women. There are tons of female-friendly places in Vegas where women can get naughty and this book will show you how to make it your playground.

LAS VEGAS TODAY

Las Vegas is a city that Americans love to hate but can't do without. Time and time again, Vegas survived by offering Americans something they couldn't find at home, such as gambling, quickie divorces, topless entertainment, and prostitution. And today they still offer all these things and more! It is a modern-day Sodom and Gomorrah.

You can get anything here and at any time of the day. Need a double-ended dildo at 2:30 a.m.? No problem. Vegas has tons of sex toy stores open all night. It's all about excess here. This city has no problem helping you find ways to spend your money.

Las Vegas has found its niche in naughtiness. It's what saved the city back in the day from becoming a dust town, and it's what makes it stand out from the rest of the cities in the world.

THE LAS VEGAS OF TOMORROW

Vegas tried its hands at promoting the city as a family destination, but that didn't last long before the city went back to its roots of promoting sex again.

There's still a lot left for Vegas, such as opening strip clubs in casinos. Why not? They already have topless shows and "toptional" pools that serve alcohol. Plus, Vegas could become the new "Porn Capital" of the world with its cheaper cost of living, production costs, open-mindedness, tax breaks, and proximity to Los Angeles.

Thanks to Nevada's early embrace of wide-open vice, Las Vegas inadvertently discovered the immense profit potential in America's forbidden desires and will continue to tap into our naughty cravings.

Naughty Travel

Welcome to Vegas

PLANNING YOUR TRIP

This book is great for visitors and locals alike. There's so much more to Las Vegas than touring casinos, shopping or hanging out poolside—unless you're topless, of course. With this book you'll discover places you've never heard of and things you never knew you could try.

This book is perfect if you're planning a week or weekend getaway to Las Vegas. Las Vegas is one of the country's naughtiest travel destinations; so whether this is your first, second, or tenth visit, make this trip your first naughty one. Even if you're a local, get out and experience the naughty side of your town.

Everyone knows that Vegas is risqué. You've seen the glitz, the decadence, and the sex on TV and film, but my book will show you how naughty Vegas really is. You'll learn all the best places to see male and female strippers, to lounge topless by the pool, to have a discreet rendezvous, where to find the naughtiest parties and more. I'll show you the sexiest hotels to stay at and what to bring with you. I'll be your naughty tour guide to Sin City. Just take my hand and get ready for a wild ride. I promise to be gentle!

WHAT TO PACK

Las Vegas is a very sexy city, and the dress code reflects that. Girls who visit Vegas tend to dress in a way they wouldn't back home. A lot of gals show off some serious cleavage, both top and bottom! The professional "working girls" often cover up more than the party-going college girls and bachelorette parties you see everywhere in Vegas. Remember that it's sexier to show less than more. And a real naughty girl doesn't reveal everything, as the mystery of what's underneath is half the thrill. Plus you'll stand out more in Vegas if you conceal instead of revealing everything for all to see.

When packing your club dresses, my advice would be to stick with dark colors, as it gets pretty wild and packed in the nightclubs and you never know when someone will spill a drink on you. Plus the more sparkles, the better. This is Las Vegas, the home of showgirls, so go all out and paint the town with as many sparkles as you want.

It's best to wear your tightest dresses the first two days you get there. Save your ruched black, or pattern dresses for days three and four, because after days of drinking and eating you'll start to feel a little bloated and these dresses will help hide it.

Let's not forget about packing your sexiest heels. Just remember that Vegas hotels are big. They are deceptively large and are always bigger than they appear from the street. The path from the lobby to your room can be a mile long—no joke. You'll be walking from casinos to nightclubs and restaurants, and you'll be dancing all night. Trust me, your feet will be sore later on, so pack some flip-flops in your purse or carry Dr. Scholl's Fast Flats (they fold up easily into your purse). Also, book a foot massage the next day at your hotel's spa. Your feet will thank you.

During the warm summer days, pack your sexiest bikini and cover-up. Lying out by the pools in Vegas is very popular, and many pool parties are like going to a nightclub in daylight. Girls even wear heels to the pool (and show up with their hair fixed and with full makeup). Pack some sexy but comfortable flats, as you'll be doing a lot of walking, and a comfortable, sexy sundress. Don't forget that the hotter it is outside, the colder it is inside the casinos. Plus a lot of the casinos won't let you walk through them with just a bathing suit on, even though they will let girls walk through their hotels at night half-naked and showing their goods, literally.

Most importantly, don't forget to pack your naughty sex toys, condoms and lube. You never know when you're going to get lucky!

PARIS HOTEL RED ROOM

NAUGHTY RENDEZVOUS

The first hotel in Las Vegas was a 126-foot-long tent on Fremont Street. Thankfully, hotels have come a long way in Sin City! If you're looking for a sexy hotel to get naughty in, then Vegas has several for you. Many of the hotels have sex toy and lingerie stores to entice thrill-seeking guests. And most hotels now have "intimacy kits" in every room that include condoms, lube, and a mini-vibrator. Plus hotels even have sexy shows, scantily clad waitresses and bartenders, and hot card dealers. You have a lot of options for naughty places to stay while visiting Las Vegas. This is a list of my favorite sexy hotels.

SEXIEST HOTELS

MANDARIN ORIENTAL
3752 S. Las Vegas Blvd.
702.590.8888
www.mandarinoriental.com/lasvegas

This dark and secluded hotel is at the City Center and is another sexy getaway spot for you and your frisky friend(s). It has won several top hotel awards (including one five-star rating from *Forbes*) and has a fantastic spa and exotic Asian décor throughout. The rooms are like mini–Zen retreats. One room, the Apex Suite, has a 270-degree view of the Strip!

ENCORE AT WYNN
3121 S. Las Vegas Blvd.
702.770.7000
www.wynnlasvegas.com

This is one of my favorite places for a girls' getaway. They have an amazing pool with these great circular divans for lounging and sharing drinks (and maybe some sneaky kisses and tickles here and there). The rooms have floor-to-ceiling windows for great views and full length mirrors next to the beds. Their tower suites have an exclusive entrance if you're on a naughty getaway and don't want a lot of prying eyes seeing you and your lover.

THE COSMOPOLITAN
3708 S. Las Vegas Blvd.
702.698.7000
www.cosmopolitanlasvegas.com

This hotel is one of the newest on the Strip and also one of the sexiest. Their three-story chandelier is an incredible sight, and the whole place is designed with an ultra-modern feel. They have some good restaurants there, such as Jaleo—a nice tapas restaurant that is reasonably priced (and look for their secret pizza place if you need a quick late-night snack). Their patio pool is gorgeous. The view of the Strip from there is fantastic, and they host concerts out on their terrace. They drain the wading pool and it becomes the dance floor for the outdoor venue. There are wraparound terrace suites, multilevel suites, and more. It's a great hotel for a girls' getaway.

FOUR SEASONS AT MANDALAY BAY
3960 S. Las Vegas Blvd.
702.632.5000
www.fourseasons.com/LasVegas

This is another great place for a lovers' getaway, or for those who don't want to be in a casino filled with drunken tourists and screaming kids. It has no gambling. You read that right, *no gambling*. This is a hotel for those who want privacy and a little luxury. It's accessed by express elevators and has only 424 rooms, many of which offer some of the best views of the Strip. If you want a place for an intimate gathering, this is the place for you.

PARIS HOTEL
3655 S. Las Vegas Blvd.
877.796.2096
www.parislasvegas.com/hotel.html

The rooms at the Paris Hotel and Casino are all lovely, but if you want to go naughty on your trip (and why wouldn't you?), book a "Red Room." These sumptuous rooms are decorated in, no surprise, sensual reds, marbles, and deep blacks. They have nice padded headboards behind the bed and, best of all, cute couches designed to look like puckered lips!

FLAMINGO HOTEL
3555 S. Las Vegas Blvd.
702.733.3111
www.flamingolasvegas.com/hotel.html

The Flamingo is one of the classic Strip hotels and casinos, and their new Go Rooms are sexy, girly, and fun. They're called "Go Rooms," because of their focus on new technology. They all have digital accessories like iPod docks, high-end televisions, stereo systems, and electronic window treatments. Their "Go with a View" rooms have great views of the Strip. The bathrooms are decorated in fun pinks and purples (much like the Flamingo's signature colors) and the rooms can be a great place to recharge all your naughty sex toys and your body after a long night.

FLAMINGO HOTEL GO ROOM

SEXIEST OFF-THE-STRIP HOTELS

RED ROCK
11011 W. Charleston Blvd.
702.797.7777
www.redrock.sclv.com

This nice place is just ten miles off the Strip, so it's great if you want to avoid the hustle and bustle of the Strip or if you're a townie looking for a hotel rendezvous with your lover or lovers. Their "twogether" package is a good deal for less than five hundred dollars. It's a two-night stay with a fifty-minute couples massage, two tickets to the movie theatre at the hotel, and a $25 breakfast voucher. The Cherry Suite will make you think you're staying in a strip club.

GREEN VALLEY RANCH
2300 Paseo Verde Pkwy., Henderson
702.617.7777
www.greenvalleyranchresort.com

This hotel is a few minutes off the Strip—in Henderson, a suburb of Las Vegas—so it's great if you're looking for a place away from the hustle and bustle. The hotel part is separate from the casino, which is great for those who don't want to walk through a casino and smell the smoke. The hotel is quiet and the entire place is decorated with simple, sexy elegance. The suites are quite nice. The living room in the Geneva Suite is big enough to hold an orgy. It even has a pool table, and you know you've always wanted to do it on one.

WESTIN LAKE LAS VEGAS RESORT & SPA
101 Montelago Blvd., Henderson
702.567.6000
www.westinlakelasvegas.com

This beautiful hotel is also in Henderson, just outside of Las Vegas, and it rests on the huge lake there. It used to be the Loews Hotel. It's very quiet and private, which is perfect if you want to get away from Las Vegas. It has no casino, but there's one right up the road if you're in the mood to gamble. It has gorgeous patio views and easy access to the golf course. The inside is Moroccan-themed, with a nice restaurant to match. It's easy to feel like you're far from America in a hotel like this, and the pool at night is very sexy. Definitely a great spot for a lovers' getaway!

SEXIEST BOUTIQUE HOTELS

RUMOR
455 E. Harmon Ave.
702.369.5400
www.rumorvegas.com

Another great place for a solo getaway, Rumor is a wild-looking place. The whole design is sort of a cross between a funhouse and a modern art museum. One room is painted in blue-and-white camouflage! Another is a two-room poolside suite that's very nice. They even have a room called the "Swinger Mega Suite," so you can imagine the stories it must have in the walls. It'd be perfect for bringing back that hottie you met while out at the pool or a night on the town.

THE ARTISAN
1501 W. Sahara Ave.
702.214.4000
www.artisanhotel.com

This place only accepts reservations Sunday through Thursday. That's because it's a constant party Friday and Saturday nights. This boutique hotel is surprisingly quiet during the week. Its gothic design feels like you've walked into a spooky mansion, but in a sexy way. Then the weekend comes and the place goes crazy. They'll have huge dubstep parties, naughty theme nights (like "Detention," during which a lot of ladies dress up like sexy schoolgirls), and wild pool parties. The rooms are all beautiful. No two are alike. The pool is European style, so feel free to go topless!

EL CORTEZ CABANA SUITES
651 E. Ogden Ave., Downtown Las Vegas
702.385.5200
www.elcortezhotelcasino.com/hotel/cabana-suites/

This place has amazing vacation packages. If you book rooms Sunday through Thursday and can get their food and gaming credits, you can pretty much get your room free. The place has a great mix of classic and modern décor. They have no resort fees. Also, guests don't pay for parking either, so that alone will save you a nice bit of money. And did I mention how sexy this hotel is for such a great price and for being downtown? Check it out for yourself.

THE ROYAL HOUSE
99 Convention Center Dr.
702.735.6117
www.royalhouselv.com

The sumptuous lobby lets you know this is going to be a nice place. They like to say that they're "close to the attractions without the distractions," and they're right. You're not far from the craziness of the Strip, but you are far enough away if it's too much for you. It was voted the hippest new place in a 2011 poll, and it's easy to see why. They blend art deco with 1970s chic, have $4.00 Jameson shots all day long, and a neat gallery of local artists in there. The rooms are nice, simple, and relaxing. It's a good place to unwind or to meet a lover or two.

SLS
2335 S. Las Vegas Blvd.
702.737.2111
www.slshotels.com/lasvegas

This new incarnation of the iconic Sahara Hotel from SLS comes with a stylish mix of Old Vegas Glamour and Modern Urban Swagger. Featuring three distinct towers, each with its own unique feel, The World, Lux and Story Towers offer over 1,600 guest rooms and 40,000 feet of mingling space. With a vibrant collection of acclaimed retailers like Fred Segal set amid award-winning, signature dining experiences, the hotel also features fabulous SLS mainstays like The Bazaar by Jose Andres and Katsuya by Starck. This hotel will stand as a true, visionary masterpiece in the world of New Vegas.

DELANO
3940 S. Las Vegas Blvd.
702.632.9444
www.delanolasvegas.com

Bringing more than a touch of the original Delano South Beach Style and service to the high-octane energy of the Strip, this new Delano Hotel provides both an intimate and high-end concept within its 43 story golden tower at the Mandalay Bay Resort Complex. With its first-class, all-suite boutique hotel experience, the Delano also features world-class accommodations like the Bathhouse Spa and Gym, alongside the contemporary, grand culinary offerings from restaurants like The Rivea, Cafe and Franklin. This is a great hotel for an intimate and sexy experience with only the best and finest that Vegas nightlife and entertainment offers.

THE CROMWELL
3595 S. Las Vegas Blvd.
702.777.3777
www.thecromwell.com

The Cromwell is the Strip's first ever, stand-alone boutique hotel, featuring 188 rooms with a luxurious, Parisian-inspired ambience. This hotel is a seductive blend of modern and vintage tastes, featuring such exclusive amenities as steam showers, hallway coffee and tea service, and Muk Bath Products. The Cromwell is also the home to GIADA, the first restaurant of celebrity and Emmy winning chef, Giada De Laurentiis. The Cromwell also features a Reserved Gaming Room and DRAI'S Nightclub—a gorgeous, 65,000 square foot Beach Club/ Nightclub that has one of the finest drink, music and dance scenes on the Strip. An absolute must!

NAUGHTY MEETUPS

There is so much naughty activity in Las Vegas that people have created social "Meetup" groups in town that cover naughty events ranging from fetish balls to sexy nightclub takeovers. Join as many as you'd like to see, even if you live out of town, as they are free. They may be planning something naughty during your next trip. Don't limit yourself to the ones I've listed. There are tons of Meetup groups in Vegas for everyone. If you're new to the city, then there are meetups for meeting men or hanging out with like-minded women. Some of the groups may not be geared towards naughtiness like the ones below, but it doesn't mean some of them can't lead into something naughty—so browse around.

LAS VEGAS TANTRA COMMUNITY
www.meetup.com/Las-Vegas-Tantra-Community

This group holds Tantra workshops, Tarot card readings, and even female orgasm workshops. Oh my! This group is great to visit solo, with your girlfriends or your lover. You never know what you may learn here!

EROTIC EXPLORATION
www.meetup.com/erotic-exploration

This group gets people together to explore adult clubs, events, and parties. If you'd feel safer checking out a strip club or a sexuality workshop for the first time with a bunch of other first-timers, this might be the group for you.

ONETASTE
www.meetup.com/OneTasteLV

This group specializes in "orgasmic meditation," in which women are stroked by clothed men in a sensual experience for both. Sound interesting? It does to me, so check them out. They also have workshops where you can become "advanced" in orgasmic meditation.

NAUGHTY DOWNTOWN

Downtown Las Vegas has a lot of charm, affordable accommodations, low-stake gambling (which is great if it's your first trip), and sexy people. It has less hustle and bustle than the Strip but keeps a lot of the glamour and a neat retro-vibe. If you want Vegas action without being crushed by tourists and having your purse emptied by expensive blackjack tables, check out downtown and all the sexy stuff it has to offer. On the next few pages you'll find all the sexiest hot spots of Downtown, handpicked by me.

GLITTER GULCH
20 Fremont St.
702.385.4774
www.glittergulch.com

This is the only strip club in downtown Las Vegas. Located on beautiful Fremont Street (Make sure to check out the light show!), this club has no cover but they do have a two-drink minimum. It recently completed a $3.5 million renovation, so it's worth a look. A lot of couples go here, so you might be able to find one feeling frisky and looking for a naughty playmate.

OSCAR'S BEEF, BOOZE & BROADS AT THE PLAZA
1 Main St.
702.386.7227
www.oscarslv.com

This appears to be a straight-up steakhouse until you notice the sexy décor and beautiful women walking around and chatting up the customers. That's because the "broads" mentioned in the name of the place are hostesses who will sit with you at dinner and talk with you during your meal. They'll tell you the best places to see shows, give you directions, make suggestions for dessert, or discuss anything from politics to sports. Don't be surprised if they're a bit flirty. The food is top-notch, and the restaurant's namesake—Oscar Goodman, who was mayor of Las Vegas for twelve years—can be seen here often. He has plenty of stories to tell and is a fountain of information about the town.

THE HIDEOUT H20 POOL AT GOLDEN NUGGET
129 Fremont St.
702.385.7111
www.goldennugget.com/LasVegas/

This is the sexiest pool in downtown Las Vegas and a hidden gem of the city. The Golden Nugget has a massive pool called "the Tank" where you can swim with exotic sea creatures. This pool is actually three levels of water, and the top has the Hideout. It's a luxurious, secluded pool with lounges for rent for $20.00. No children under 16 are admitted, so it's usually nothing but college kids and adults up there. You can relax and watch that hot co-ed take a dive while you sip a mimosa.

ICE BAR AT GOLDEN NUGGET
129 Fremont St.
702.385.7111
www.goldennugget.com/LasVegas/

Located not far from the Golden Nugget's Tank and Hideout H20 Pool, the Ice Bar is a sexy place for cocktails. It has floor-to-ceiling windows that look out at the pool, but it somehow feels secluded. Their vodka collection is outstanding and it's a fine place to lounge between swims or action at the tables. The all-white décor makes the place feel a bit otherworldly and the pool views are delicious. You can sip a martini while you watch the hotties and decide which one to bring here for a drink later.

EL CORTEZ CABANA SUITES

651 E. Ogden Ave.
702.385.5200
www.elcortezhotelcasino.com/hotel/cabana-suites/

This is the sexiest boutique hotel in downtown Las Vegas. It's full of stunning design. It feels like a Strip hotel that got picked up by a giant and placed onto Fremont Street. They have four exotic suites designed by interior design contest winners that range in themes from American mobster to 1950s retro. Their other rooms are painted in exotic greens and ultra-modern furnishings. If you want to feel chic while hanging out downtown, stay here.

COMMONWEALTH

525 E. Fremont St.
702.445.6400
www.commonwealthlv.com

The Commonwealth is a classic testament to the East Coast, speakeasy, pub-style bars of yesterday, located in the burgeoning, new hip district of Downtown Las Vegas. Offering superb service, high-class entertainment and a comfortable atmosphere, the Commonwealth has quickly become a beacon for locals and tourists alike. One can sit high above on the second floor and look out over the swinging neon haze of Fremont Street from the Rooftop Bar, surrounded by glass chandeliers and tasteful vintage art from days long gone. This is an excellent place for bringing friends or a special date.

Naughty by Day

SEXY DAY TOURS

There are plenty of tour services in the city, and plenty of them are naughty. Tours are great if you're tired of the typical tourist attractions, walking through the casinos, and seeing the same shows over and over. Tours are great even for frequent visitors to Las Vegas and locals. You can often discover things about the city you didn't know.

Most people think that all the naughtiness in Las Vegas begins at night, but that's not true at all. There are lots of naughty things to do during the day. Vegas isn't called "Sin City" for nothing. You can sin twenty-four hours a day, seven days a week here. Naughtiness shouldn't be something you just turn on at night. If you're a real naughty girl it should be on all the time!

The great thing about Vegas is that if you're not into staying up late, drinking at the bars, or going to clubs, you can still get into naughty trouble during the day with the following suggestions on the next few pages.

LOVE CLOUD
4080 Paradise Rd. #15
702.267.7499
www.lovecloudvegas.com

"What happens over Vegas stays over Vegas!" Love Cloud is a private plane that offers you the opportunity to join the Mile High Club with your lover or for a "swinging" good time. You can either book a flight during the day or at night, depending on when you want to get naughty. Visit their website for more details on their plane and limo packages, along with add-ons to make your experience even naughtier. Feel free to bring your own food, drinks and music, then just lay back and enjoy "the ride" on their comfy bed.

GONDOLA RIDES AT THE VENETIAN
3355 S. Las Vegas Blvd.
702.414.1000
www.venetian.com

Maybe you'll never make a trip to Venice to ride a gondola, but Las Vegas makes a lot of money by turning your fantasies into reality. The Venetian Hotel and Casino is so large that it has a shopping mall in it . . . with a canal that runs through it. They have gondoliers on staff to guide you through the hotel. You can have a sexy ride through the Venetian with your lover. They have rides both inside the casino and outside the hotel. The outside rides offer beautiful views of the Strip, especially at night. The inside rides are quieter, and are a nice way to get away from the hustle and bustle for a little while.

EIFFEL TOWER RIDE AT PARIS HOTEL
3655 S. Las Vegas Blvd.
702.946.7000
www.parislasvegas.com

Maybe you can't make it to the Eiffel Tower in Paris, France, but you can go to the Paris casino in Las Vegas. They have a stunning replica of the Eiffel Tower there. It's half the size of the original, but you're still fifty stories high! From the top of the tower you can watch the fountain show at Bellagio, which is a very sexy show to watch (because, let's be honest, it's incredibly phallic). Visit solo or with your lover to feel a little naughty!

JUBILEE BACKSTAGE TOUR AT BALLY'S
3645 S. Las Vegas Blvd.
702.967.4938
www.ballyslasvegas.com/things-to-do/jubilee-backstage-tours.html

The Jubilee showgirls are sexy enough on stage, but they're even sexier when you're walking next to them backstage! For just a small fee, you get to see the sexy girls that were just parading around topless on stage up close and personal. One of them (who, sadly, won't be topless) guides you on an all-access backstage tour. You get to see the beautiful costumes, marvel at the incredible sets (not to mention see hunky stagehands moving them around), ask your tour guide any questions you want, and you get to see a lot of sexy ladies. These tours are only available Monday, Wednesday and Saturday at 11 a.m.

BROTHEL TOURS

It's a common misconception that prostitution is legal in Las Vegas. It is not. However, it *is* legal in certain parts of Nevada, including some counties that are a quick day trip away. Rent a car (or a limo) and drive to one of the legal brothels. In some of them you can take pictures, buy souvenirs, have a drink at the bar, or take a tour to see what a real brothel is like. You can easily visit many of the brothels by taking a tour without taking part in sexual activities. Of course, there are . . . other activities you can engage in if you're willing and have the cash. Below are a list of some of the brothels to check out. Visit the websites for a list of girls available and to contact them about touring their brothel.

www.chickenranchbrothel.com
www.bunnyranch.com
www.mustangranchbrothel.com
www.sherisranch.com

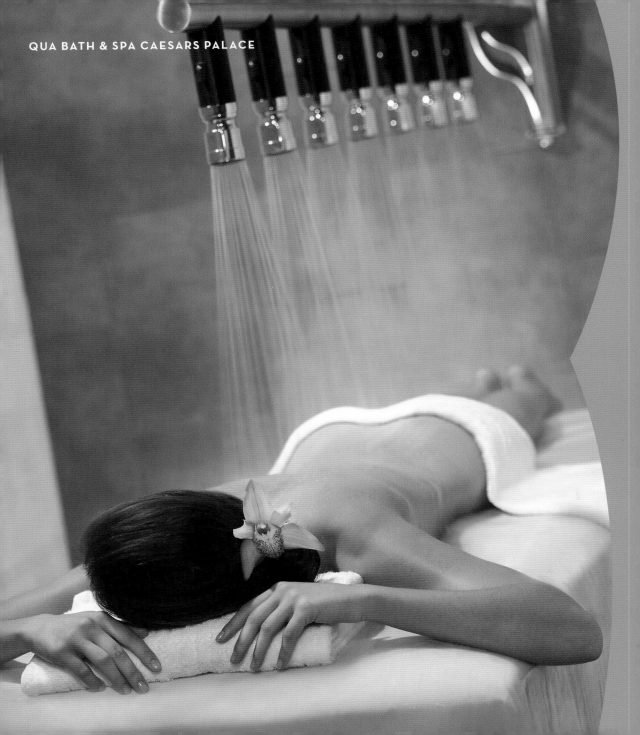

QUA BATH & SPA CAESARS PALACE

SEXIEST SPAS

Las Vegas isn't all about wild nightlife and debauchery! It's also a great place to pamper and pleasure yourself with a variety of wonderfully naughty erotic massage services and spa treatments. With so much to choose from, there's something here for everyone.

Let's face it, Las Vegas can be exhausting, especially after a long night of partying! What better way to relax and unwind than with a fabulous spa treatment or erotic massage. Spa days are great for a solo trip, a girl's getaway or a naughty treat for you and your lover to share. On the next few pages you'll find some of the sexiest spas and erotic massage services that Las Vegas has to offer.

QUA BATH & SPA CAESARS PALACE

RED ROCK HOTEL SPA
11011 W. Charleston Blvd.
702.797.7777
www.redrock.sclv.com

Named one of the top 100 spas by *Conde Nast* magazine, the spa at the Red Rock Hotel is a great place to get away from the craziness of the Strip. They offer discounts for locals, and sexy treatments like the Island Glow (which uses coconut oil and "exotic nut extracts," which sounds kind of naughty). They also have river rafting, horseback riding, and rock climbing expeditions.

SAHRA SPA & HAMMAM AT COSMOPOLITAN
3708 S. Las Vegas Blvd.
702.698.7000
www.cosmopolitanlasvegas.com

The Cosmopolitan is right in the middle of the Strip and one of the newest casino hotels. As a result, it has one of the newest and finest spas. You can book a private spa suite for up to eight people. What better way to host a bachelorette party? Their Moonflower Ritual treatment is amazing, a warm jasmine rose clay wrap followed by an oil massage. Don't miss out on the hammam—a massive heated stone slab where you can get oil and soap massages. You won't want to get off it.

SPA AT ENCORE
3131 S. Las Vegas Blvd.
702.770.4772
www.wynnlasvegas.com

This has to be one of the sexiest spas in Las Vegas. This opulent spa looks like something from the lost city of Shangri-La. It's a *Forbes* five-star award-winner, and for good reason. You'll feel like royalty just by walking into the place. They also have a full salon with reasonable prices for manicures, pedicures, and other treatments. Check out their Choco Latte Body Buff!

RELIQUARY SPA AND SALON AT HARD ROCK
4455 Paradise Rd.
702.693.5000
www.hardrockhotel.com

This spa is off the Strip, but still a lot of fun and sexy. They have a gorgeous pool area and one of the most upscale and sensuous juice bars I've seen. You can get alcohol and coffee there, too, but the juice drinks are so luxurious (and good for you!) that you'll want to indulge in them. Reliquary offers a variety of good skin treatments and massages, including a specialized reflexology massage and a Drum Sticks massage where they use bamboo reeds to tap, drum, and roll all over your body. Be warned, if you have a caning fetish, you might enjoy it a little too much!

QUA BATH & SPA AT CAESARS PALACE
3570 S. Las Vegas Blvd.
702.731.7110
www.caesarspalace.com

Qua is the top-ranked spa in the city. They keep up the Roman tradition of purifying baths with their three different pools of varying sizes and temperatures to reinvigorate you. You can also get a Crystal Body Art treatment—a shower, scrub, and a personalized crystal body art session. Why not give your body some sexy bling? Check out their Arctic Ice Room, which, believe it or not, has falling snow in it. Feeling frisky? Book their Sweet Romance for Two package, which includes a private shower for two!

EROTIC MASSAGES

XOXO GENEVIEVE SENSUAL MASSAGE
www.xoxogenevieve.com

Genevieve is a fully licensed massage therapist who fuses several unique massage disciplines together to create a fulfilling awakening of the Kundalini Spirit within you. Taking her cues from Qigong, Tantra, Swedish and the Thai massage arts, Genevieve is able to craft a sensual bodywork session that is personalized and healing, helping you to create a more powerful flow of energy throughout your mind and body. Her sessions are professional and

QUA BATH & SPA CAESARS PALACE

superbly relaxing, as she engages her deep knowledge of the Tantric Arts to deliver you to unknown heights of erotically charged bliss. Genevieve is a true jewel of Tantric Therapy in Sin City!

AAA TANTRA MASSAGE

www.aaatantramassage.com

Come and see what Sahara, the expert in all healing, tantric body-work massage arts, can do for you at AAA Tantra Massage. Known as the "black tigress in the desert", this self-proclaimed Initiatress of Pleasure offers a variety of massage packages for discerning customers looking to awaken the power of their sexual health and being through the course of ancient Tantric Rites and Methods. Practicing massage and erotically charged healing for twelve years, Sahara is a skilled practitioner with a charming and professional personality. She offers a variety of massage options along with the most magical variations of mini spa treatments, designed to titillate and delight the senses towards Deep Relaxation and Pleasure.

TOA TANTRA

www.toatantra.org

TOA Tantra is the perfect place to find a fabulous couples massage, as they offer a variety of treatments and styles, all of which are firmly grounded in the sacred spirituality of the Tantra. TOA works with a group of therapists who are trained not only in Tantric Bodywork but also Reiki, Hypnossage, and Shiatsu Deep Tissue therapies. It is possible to book more than one therapist for couples massage or for those who are exploring tantric bodywork for the educational experience. With a beautiful and professional staff, TOA is dedicated to enhancing your pleasure, relaxation and helping to release the stress of your day through the massage and body experience of a lifetime!

ZENTASTIC TANTRA MASSAGE LAS VEGAS
www.azentastictantramassage.com

One of the finest and most zentastic massages to be found in Las Vegas, the Zentastic Tantra Massage experience brought to you by Sahara, is a truly mind blowing and therapeutic fountain of enhanced relaxation and pleasure. Utilizing a treasure trove of tools and knowledge taken from the erotic arts, Sahara is able to sustain your pleasure with tantric techniques and help you to awaken the sacred Kundalini energy within. With a wide selection of massage options, she uses aromatherapies, oils, toys and her own unique sense of empathetic improvisation to customize a massage experience that is tailor-made to satiate your wildest desires. Come and be tamed by this "Black Tigress of the Desert" and you will surely be coming back for more!

RUBDOWN BY ROSE LAS VEGAS TANTRA MASSAGE
www.rubdownbyrose.com

Rose is a knowledgeable and gifted tantric massage therapist and she is perfect for couples who wish to explore the methods of tantric massage together. Rose's sessions are breathtaking, erotically charged journeys into mutual touch and she loves to entertain curious couples who are seeking to spice up their lives with a bit of intimate relaxation. Offering several different packages, she is a skilled masseuse who happens to be stunningly sexy! Check out her website if you or your significant other are interested in having a spiritually invigorating and completely relaxing experience by the hands of an artfully talented and beautiful woman.

LAS VEGAS TANTRA MASSAGE
www.fullbodytantra.com

Step into a complete and total world of blissful relaxation with Kimberly at Las Vegas Tantra Massage. Kimberly specializes in nude sensual tantric massage and uses a variety of start and stop tantric techniques to help you relax and prolong your pleasure. Kimberly also offers a great course which she calls "Female 101", which teaches you how to truly please a woman and drive her completely wild—satisfaction guaranteed! Kimberly has a stunning and instinctive way of reading what your body needs while in the midst of a massage and tailoring the experience just for you. Come and see this talented massage artist for yourself and be prepared to experience the Divine.

HOT VEGAS TOUCH
www.hotvegastouch.com

Hot Vegas Touch may be the hottest outcall massage service in Las Vegas, catering to high rollers, business executives and the world traveler set. With a variety of "goddesses" to choose from, Hot Vegas Touch certainly delivers only the finest, most professional and courteous massage packages. Hot Vegas Touch is not only aimed at men, but women and couples alike are encouraged to book a private massage with these talented therapists for a night that you won't soon forget. Couples whose sex lives has fallen into the doldrums of routine may find that a uniquely erotic tantric massage that is personalized for you by a trained therapist will invigorate and rekindle the flames of romance!

NAUGHTY EVENTS

There are many reasons to visit Vegas (like you really need another one apart from all the hedonism that goes on there), but if you're looking for something different for your next visit why not check out one of their many naughty trade shows throughout the year?

There are lots of naughty conventions and trade shows in the city. Sex is one of the coins of the realm, so it's no surprise that Las Vegas has huge shows devoted to it.

The city has a naughty tradeshow for about everything you can imagine. There are shows for swingers, leather fetishists, adult film studios, strippers, dominants and submissives, sex toys, and more. If you have a turn-on, Las Vegas has a trade show for it. If you're involved in any kind of adult-themed business, there's a show for you.

To find out more and to plan your next trip (or maybe you're a local looking for something different to do), check out my suggestions over the next pages.

ADULT ENTERTAINMENT EXPO (JANUARY)
www.adultentertainmentexpo.com

It shouldn't be a surprise that many Las Vegas conventions are for naughty professions, or for the fans that love them. The biggest, of course, is the Adult Entertainment Expo. This is sometimes known as "the AVN's" because the convention is sponsored by (among many others) the *Adult Video News* publication. This is the premiere adult entertainment convention in the country. It's every January and it draws thousands over the course of the weekend. The show also has sex-toy vendors to help you discover some new naughty items for the bedroom and your lover. Almost every major porn star is there, and many up-and-comers are there to be seen. There are seminars on how to break into the business, how to dominate your lover, and everything else under the sun. Where else can you meet your favorite porn star, buy a life-size sex doll of her, and have her sign it?

AVN AWARDS (JANUARY)
http://avnawards.avn.com/

The AEE is also host to the AVN Awards. You can buy tickets for this event, but get them early because they will sell out. You'll see all of your favorite porn stars dressed to the nines and you never know who might be sitting next to you. It could be the girl who wins for "Best Anal" scene or a Hollywood or sports celebrity, as they sometimes come to the show. The show draws big names to the stage, as they get big-time comedians and famous singers to host it. Plus it's hard not to be entertained throughout the awards show with some of the award titles—"Best Threesome," "Best Blowjob," and "Best Anal," to name a few.

ELECTRIC DAISY CARNIVAL LAS VEGAS (JUNE)
www.electricdaisycarnival.com

Every year, the Electric Daisy Carnival comes to Las Vegas, where a community of the decidedly (and dedicatedly) hip and cool come together underneath the glow of an electric sky to celebrate the power of individuality, love, art and transcendence. A three-day weekend, the EDC is a madcap romp at the Las Vegas Speedway that takes you through a hyper-charged atmosphere of lights, big-spectacle theater and dance. Music fills every inch of space and you can strike sparks anywhere, as thousands descend to participate in this ultimate celebration of spirit. Beautiful people are everywhere! Girls, scantily clad, wearing pasties and body paint and men dressed in fantastic outfits flood this modern Mecca of cool. Recommended are the Special VIP tickets which ensure an all-access experience, including VIP dinner, table service and parking.

INTERNEXT (JANUARY)
www.internext-expo.com

Do you run an adult website? Do you want to start one? If so, you need to visit InterNext, a convention presented by *AVN Online* and dedicated to the wild world of Internet sex. This show has a lot of seminars on building website traffic, advertising, website design, and much more. They also have a great after-party called the GFY Party, as in "Go Fuck Yourself" party. How can you miss with a name like that?

LAS VEGAS INTERNATIONAL LINGERIE SHOW (MARCH & SEPTEMBER)
www.lvlingerieshow.com

This is a great place to see a lot of sexy gals in lingerie, and to buy a lot for you. Imagine what a great girls' getaway it would be: you and your friends exploring all the corsets, bras, panties, and stockings, and picking out what to wear to an exotic nightclub or perhaps back at the hotel room for a private show of your own. This show has a heavy emphasis on adult lingerie, nightclub fashions, and items for exotic dancers, but they also have daywear, pajamas, and other fun stuff for sexy lounging.

ADULT NOVELTY EXPO (JANUARY)
www.noveltyexpo.com

It's an entire show dedicated to sex toys and other sexy products. Add it to your girls' getaway weekend for a trip you'll never forget. If you have a business selling naughty toys at parties, you owe it to yourself to come to this expo. They have a good number of adult performers there as celebrity endorsers, and there are plenty of free samples to stuff your purse!

GENTLEMEN'S CLUB OWNERS EXPO (AUGUST)
www.edpublications.com

Like strip clubs? Want to open one, or even just work in one? Check out the Gentlemen's Club Owners Expo. This show celebrated its twentieth anniversary in 2012 and has become the biggest exotic club event in the country. They offer seminars on legal issues, attracting customers, and even D.J.-ing. As you can imagine, the after-parties for this show are full of beautiful dancers strutting their stuff in hopes of landing premiere spots at the best clubs.

NUDIST CLUBHOUSE EXPO (JUNE)
www.nudistexpo.com

This isn't just a place to see naked people. Located at the Alexis Park Hotel (across the street from the Hard Rock), it's an entire convention dedicated to the nudist lifestyle. You have to wear clothes at the Alexis, but they have a "nude hotel" five miles away. They have nude pool parties there each night of the expo. You can still attend them if you're not staying there; just get your tickets for them when you register for the expo. They even have nudist glow-in-the-dark mini-golf outings! The nudist lifestyle isn't for everyone, but if you're inclined to check it out, or are already living it, this is the event for you.

KINKY KARNIVAL (JULY)

www.kinkykarnivallv.com

If you're looking for something kinky, then check out the Kinky Karnival. It's a charity event benefiting the Las Vegas HIV Outreach Center and has a heavy fetish theme. Rubber, leather, dominance, submission, latex, you name it; it's all here and all for a lovely charity. There's a silent auction to benefit the HIV Outreach Center where you can bid on floggers, canes, cock-ball torture weights, and more erotic items. They have some delightfully naughty activities there, like the Dildo Ring Toss, the Flogging Booth, and even a Principal's Office in case you've been bad and need some discipline.

FETISH AND FANTASY HALLOWEEN BALL (OCTOBER)

www.halloweenball.com

This kinky event is held at the Hard Rock Hotel Casino every year. There are many Halloween-themed events in Las Vegas, but this is the biggest and best. It has been recommended by travel websites and the Travel Channel as one of the premiere events in the city. They have a strict dress code, so make sure you meet it before you show up there. Book early, because this event will sell out. There are a lot of people who like to dress up in rubber, PVC, Saran Wrap, and a lot of other kinky material, and they love to show off their stuff, so make sure you come prepared.

VEGAS SIN
4500 W. Tropicana Ave.
702.287.7777 / 888.234.2334
www.lflus.com/lasvegassin

Las Vegas' Legacy Football League team (which used to be known as the Lingerie Football League) brings sexy, strong women to the gridiron at the Orleans Arena. If you're looking for something fun to do with your lover, why not treat him to a game of sexy football played by beautiful, strong women?

SHEDONISM (SEPTEMBER)
www.shedonismlasvegas.com

Ready to indulge your curiosity about other girls? If you're looking to cross the bi-curious bridge, this is one of the best events to do it at. It's an all-girl resort takeover event that usually occurs in late summer or early autumn. If you're a girl who likes girls, or are just coming out of your shell, this event is an amazing time that takes place over five days. They have a pride parade, pool party, bands, D.J.s, and much, much more.

MIDSUMMER LINGERIE MASQUERADE
www.palms.com/midsummer

Held at the Palms Casino Hotel, this annual party brings out sexy people in exotic masks to party and get freaky without having to worry about others knowing who they are. It's centered at the Palms Pool, and everyone is encouraged to dress in their best lingerie and to grab a mask so they can let down their inhibitions. It has a wonderful Rio Carnivale–type of feel to it, so everyone's dancing and feeling great.

LAS VEGAS SALSA CONGRESS (JULY)

www.mysalsacongress.com/las-vegas

This is a huge, annual salsa event, located at the Tropicana. It has over forty workshops for you to learn the craft. They also have a big salsa dance party every night to show off your new moves, shake your booty, and possibly meet that sexy Latino guy (if only for a night). Be sure to check out their team competition for amazing choreography and so many sexy dancers that you'll lose count of them. If you love salsa dancing, you can't afford to miss it.

LAS VEGAS BELLY DANCE INTENSIVE AND FESTIVAL (SEPTEMBER)

www.bellydanceintensive.com

If you prefer belly dance to salsa, check out this festival held in September at the Flamingo. Belly dancing is a sexy art form. It's also a great way to get into shape and to build confidence in your body. You can learn sexy moves for your lover or to use on the dance floor to attract a lover. The festival is a four-day convention of belly dancers of all skill levels, with workshops, parties, and shopping. You can buy all sorts of beautiful belly-dancing outfits there, and the eye candy is outstanding.

LAS VEGAS CHOCOLATE FESTIVAL AND PASTRY SHOW
www.sincitychocolatefestival.com

If you want to indulge your sweet tooth, be sure to attend this decadent show. It's a one-day event and is your opportunity to taste sinful treats made by some of the best pastry chefs and chocolatiers in the city. It's a great activity for you and your lover. Just imagine tasting all those sweet treats together. Don't forget that chocolate is an aphrodisiac, so make sure to buy some to take back to your hotel room (where you can serve them on your lover's tummy . . . or other body parts). It benefits St. Jude's Children's Hospital, and tickets sell out fast, so don't wait to get yours.

RED CARPET TANGO FESTIVAL (OCTOBER)
www.redcarpettangofestival.com

Not much is sexier on the dance floor than two people doing the tango. This four-day festival celebrating the erotic ballroom dance takes place at the Las Vegas Hotel and Casino. There are many workshops there (over thirty hours' worth) taught by some of the finest instructors in the world. The musicians are just as skilled as the dance instructors, and are known worldwide for their skill. If you and your lover want to thrill each other and bring some intense heat to the dance floor (and the bedroom), don't miss this event.

VEGAS EXCHANGE (AUGUST)
www.vegasexchange.com

If you're interested in adding some spice to your bedroom by adding a third, fourth, or fifth person to the mix, you might want to check out this event dedicated to the swinging lifestyle held at the Palms Casino Resort. It features a "Moroccan Interlude Under the Stars" party one night and a masquerade party on another. They have celebrity guest speakers, couples' workshops on everything from erotic massage to electro-stimulation, a pool-party bikini contest, and even workshops on how to open and run your own swingers' club.

BURLESQUE HALL OF FAME WEEKEND (MAY/JUNE)
www.bhofweekend.com

This event celebrates the art of the tease and taking it off. It features pool-side fashion shows, red-carpet photo ops, workshops—and more feather boas, sparkles, and pasties than you can imagine. If you like girls who bring the va-voom, or you want to be one of those girls, then be sure to check out this show. This event is great if you're looking for some clean, naughty fun in Vegas. Remember that naughty doesn't always have to be about being naked. Sometimes a nice tease is just as naughty.

VIVA LAS VEGAS (APRIL)
www.vivalasvegas.net

This bills itself as "the biggest rockabilly party in the world." They may be right. The festival (usually held in the spring) hosts not only quality rockabilly bands from all over the world, it also has a classic muscle car show, tattoo parlor, and some of the loveliest burlesque performers on the planet. The Tiki Pool Party lasts three days and features a vintage swimwear competition. There are burlesque dance and makeup classes, a burlesque showcase featuring some of the best dancers around, and Burlesque Bingo!

LAS VEGAS BURLESQUE SPECTACULAR
www.lvburlesquefest.com

This annual fall festival highlights all things shimmy and shake. It has dozens of performers from around the world (including some from local strip clubs and topless shows at Strip casino hotels), special events at multiple hotels, three nights of performances, and a burlesque procession down Fremont Street and under the bright lights to the Burlesque Hall of Fame.

FETISH EVENTS

SIN IN THE CITY
www.sin-in-the-city.com

This annual event is one of the bigger kink events in the Las Vegas leather community. It is dedicated to leather fetishists, the BDSM lifestyle, rope bondage, and all things hardcore kink. They host the Southwest Olympus Leather contest and have some excellent bootblacks working hard to please! There are all sorts of workshops on kinks and fetishes, so it's a great place to learn something new for the bedroom.

FOOTNIGHT LAS VEGAS
www.footnight.com/vegas.html

Yes, these events are dedicated to foot worship. If you like feet, or want special attention paid to yours, these events are amazing. They offer one-on-one play areas, gorgeous ladies, and plenty of pretty feet. Visit their website to find out their next event. And why not bring your lover so you can play together.

POWER EXCHANGE
www.powerexchange.com/las_vegas.html

This swingers' club requires a paid membership, but you can be assured of privacy (no cameras or cell phones allowed), condom use, and a fun time in their exotic lounges and playrooms. They cater to couples, single men, single women, and trans-girls. They host a special event night every third Saturday, and their club is full of fun places. They have a full dungeon, exotic bedrooms, a geisha lounge, and even a "comic lounge" where you can play out your superhero fantasies.

NAUGHTY SEX CLASSES

Why not get a little educated on your next trip to Vegas? It can be your little secret! Sex is, of course, all over Las Vegas, so it's no surprise that there are many opportunities in town to improve your techniques and sexual education.

You can attend one of the many classes offered or host your own naughty education party with one of the sex-toy parties. This is a fun way to get your girlfriends together for some naughty fun. It can be something fun you do over drinks to put you in a frisky mood for when you head out on the town, or to keep yourself busy during the day while your lover is out playing golf or gambling. Maybe you'll end up bringing one of your new toys with you for that lucky guy you take home or back to your hotel room! If you're a local, can you think of a better way to surprise your lover than with something new you've learned in time for their birthday?

NIKKI LUNDBERG
www.nikkilundberg.com

Nikki Lundberg not only has gorgeous hair, but she's a certified sex coach who can help you reclaim the fire in your relationship and learn about your sexual nature. She holds a "sex talk party" for women once a month. Why not schedule one for you and your girlfriends? Who knows what you might learn?

BARBARA CARRELLAS
www.barbaracarrellas.com

Barbara Carrellas is the founder of Urban Tantra, which encourages the merging of our spiritual and erotic lives. She teaches many classes on everything from dominance and submission, erotic breathing, and even how to throw a great sex party!

TANTRESSA VEGA
702.340.9881
www.tantressavega.com

Come and experience the magical and mythical power of Tantressa Vega as she takes you on a journey into the Tantric Arts of sacred sexuality and sensual awareness. Tantressa is an intuitive healer, teacher and gifted tantric massage practitioner who also makes breathtaking works of visual art inspired by her spiritual process. She is here to teach and heal and offers a variety of different packages with different modalities all geared to helping you become more aware of the sensual being inside you that yearns to be healed.

SEXY-AS-YOU-ARE : LAS VEGAS ROMANCE WORKSHOPS
www.lasvegasbacheloretteworkshop.com

Sexy-As-You-Are workshops are an absolutely perfect function for your bachelorette party or really, ANY kind of Naughty Girls Night Out. Sexy-As-You-Are is the brainchild of Heidi, an everyday kind of gal with a keen interest in sex education and all things sex related. She started these workshops so that women could gather together in a fun, safe and friendly environment to speak openly about sex in a non-judgmental atmosphere. She offers several different sex-themed workshops and each is interactive, including demonstrations and practice (on fun props, of course!). Check it out and see which workshop is right for you and your girls!

MISTRESSES

MISTRESS KIKKO
702.994.1872
www.mistresskikkolasvegas.com

This Asian goddess demands your worship, so you'd better be serious before calling Mistress Kikko. Her seventy-five-minute sessions will leave you whimpering for more. She welcomes novice and pro subs, so just let her know your experience level and then hang on for the ride.

SHERI'S RANCH
10551 Homestead Rd., Pahrump
702.387.0500
www.sherisranch.com

This brothel has special Mistress packages, including a "Femdom Party" in which Sheri's Mistress will make you submit to her authority. They also have a BDSM toy session, in which you'll be teased, whipped, spanked, and tortured with everything from ice cubes to riding crops.

LADY ICE QUEEN
702.882.4361
www.ladyicequeen.com

There's nothing cold about Lady Ice Queen. She's a hot dominatrix who can teach you how to dominate your lover and become that powerful figure they desire. Or, if you prefer, she can teach you to be a proper slave and know your place. She has a fully stocked dungeon, so be ready for an intense session.

SARAH BLAKE - THE LITTLE MISTRESS
www.thelittlemistress.com

Get ready for the most intense domme experience in all of Las Vegas with Mistress Sarah Blake! Sarah is a talented and versatile erotic art professional whose dedication to pleasure and pain in a safe and professional environment is unrivaled in Sin City. She is a willing and able guide, helping you to achieve the most satisfaction possible from your wildest and sexiest fantasies. She is currently in the process of building a fully functional BDSM Dungeon in Vegas and is looking forward to seeing you. Come and experience this talented vixen for yourself. You will be duly rewarded!

EROTIC PHOTOGRAPHERS

You come to Vegas and take photos of your holiday, but why not get a private photo shoot to share with your lover(s) or just for yourself? You can even hire any of these photographers to go out on a night with you to take photos of your bachelorette party, girlfriends getaway, or just because you're fabulous. You can even hire them for a private session with your lover. You can bring them to your hotel room, visit their studio, or head to the desert for an erotic shoot. The photographers specialize in photos from fetish, boudoir, erotic, nude, semi-nude, pinup, burlesque, and more. You just need to find the one that suits you.

LA MARIE PORTRAITURE
918.606.4979
www.lamarieportraiture.com

This studio just relocated to Las Vegas in 2013 from Tulsa, Oklahoma. They have an *all-female* team, along with hair and makeup artists, and will treat you to champagne and chocolates during your session. They offer boudoir, couples, bachelorette, and boudoir party packages.

ORCATEK BOUDOIR
702.482.8393
www.boudoirphotographerlasvegas.com

They are based in Arizona but shoot every month in Vegas, so make sure to plan in advance. Orcatek loves subtle sexuality and tastefully erotic images. If you want some sexy photos but want to make sure they won't be over the top, you might find the right photographer here. They offer books, calendars, prints and posters of your photos, which make a great gift for yourself or your lover.

LAS VEGAS PHOTO FANTASY
702.608.2274
www.lasvegasphotofantasy.com

Marcos Rivera has worked with adult film stars and exotic models from all over the world, so you know you'll be in good hands with him. If you want stuff that's a little more hardcore, give him a call.

LA MARIE PORTRAITURE

HAUTE SHOTS
10624 S. Eastern Ave. Suite A-141
Henderson
www.hauteshots.net

If you'd prefer a woman taking naughty photos of you, you can't do much better than Stacie Frazier of Haute Shots. She loves to "unleash your inner supermodel," so check out her website to see all that she offers.

LAS VEGAS STUDIOS
www.lasvegasstudios.com

John and Christine Copeland can make you look fabulous. John's the photographer and Christine is the makeup artist and hair stylist. John has over thirty years experience and loves glamour photography. They offer many different styles, so you have a lot of fun options at their studio. Want some lovely glamour photos for a modeling resume or acting portfolio? They have you covered. Want something more risqué? They can do that, too. They excel at boudoir photography. John was a photographer for *Penthouse* and *Playboy* for many years.

I SEE SEXY
702.595.3688
www.iseesexy.com

This studio is fairly new on the scene, but already making waves with their great photos and love of pinup photography. They also love shooting bachelorette parties and women of all shapes. Plus they have five stars on Yelp, which is hard to get, so you know you're in good hands with them.

HOT SHOTS PHOTOGRAPHY OF LAS VEGAS
4390 S. Valley View Blvd. Suite #220
702.743.5957
www.hotshotsphoto.info

Specializing in all forms of portrait, boudoir and glamour photography, Robert Anthony has been a professional photographer for over forty years. Whatever you dare to dream, Robert can make those dreams come true in vivid and stunning images that you can treasure for a lifetime. Taking inspiration directly from portrait photography legends Laslo Willinger and George Hurrell of the '30s and '40s, Robert has a keen eye and master's touch. In a comfortable and relaxed environment, Hot Shots takes boudoir photography to new, sultry heights as they set the stage for your wildest flights of fancy.

SEXY DANCE CLASSES

Las Vegas is known for many things: gambling, sex, booze, neon, excess, and dancing. The strip-club industry is huge in Las Vegas. Strip-club owners hold their annual convention there. Dancing girls are everywhere you look. They are in the windows of casinos, on stages above blackjack tables, in cages at fetish-themed parties, and even on sidewalks outside Strip casinos.

As you can imagine, you can find any kind of dancing style you want in a city like Las Vegas. That means you can learn any kind of style you want. If you're going to spend an extended time there, why not learn an exotic form of dance? If you see some sexy moves at a strip club and would like to show them off to your lover, you can learn them here. You can learn everything from stripping to fire dancing; so don't miss the opportunity of what Naughty Vegas has to offer.

STRIPTEASE, LAP-DANCING, AND POLE-DANCING CLASSES

STRIPPER 101 AT PLANET HOLLYWOOD
3663 Las Vegas Blvd.
702.260.7200
www.stripper101.com

They claim to offer the "#1 pole-dancing class in the world." Their basic class is seventy-five minutes of instruction from some of the city's top dancers. They also offer a "VIP" package that gets you a complimentary cocktail and a ticket to a show (even Chippendale's if you want!). The "What Women Want" package gets you a complimentary souvenir photo and a V-Card, which gets you into many nightclubs and strip bars around town for free!

NIGHT SCHOOL FOR GIRLS
702.701.7778
www.nightschool4girls.com

They have a wonderfully naughty name and offer some great packages for a girls' night out. Their Preferred Package includes a seventy-minute class, diploma, photos, free admission to six different nightclubs, and free drinks or open bar at all of them. The "Ultimate" package gets you all of that and a free ticket to the Thunder from Down Under male-stripper show with reserved seating. Yum!

POLE DANCING LAS VEGAS
702.420.0406
www.poledancinglasvegas.net

They are highly rated and have a great bachelorette party package that includes seventy-five minutes of pole, go-go, and burlesque dancing instruction and VIP admittance to two nightclubs of your choice, such as Tao and Chateau. They also sell poles for your home. Perfect souvenir from Vegas!

MEN OF SAPPHIRE POLE-DANCING CLASSES
3025 Industrial Rd.
702.796.6000
www.menofsapphire.com/pole-dancing/

They were voted best gentleman's club in 2012 by a *Las Vegas Review Journal* poll. They also happen to offer erotic dance classes. What better place to learn stripping than in a famous strip club? Classes start at $35.00, but why not spend $60.00 and get admission to their male strip show added to the deal? They have a four-girl minimum to put on a class, so keep that in mind.

POLE FITNESS STUDIO
4265 S. Arville St., Suite A
702.878.7653
www.polefitnessstudio.com

This studio was voted #1 by locals on Yelp.com. They have two different pole-dancing studios and can even create a third if they need it. They have workshops and can be booked for private parties. Their classes can take you from "Flirting" level to "Queen" level of mastery. They have a "Cougar Pole" class for women over thirty-five and a "Booty Pole" class that will strengthen your booty while taking you through levels one and two of their pole-dance classes.

LAS VEGAS STRIPPER POLES
4305 S. Dean Martin Dr., Suite 110
702.360.3756
www.lasvegasstripperpoles.com

They offer basic to advanced pole-dancing classes, chair techniques, and even classes on how to dance in stiletto heels. Or you can attend Vegas Stripper University, which is an interactive show. You can also rent a pole and have it delivered to your hotel room or house for a naughty girls' party of your own. They're conveniently located right off the Strip near the Rio Casino Hotel.

BURLESQUE CLASSES

X BURLESQUE UNIVERSITY AT FLAMINGO
3555 S. Las Vegas Blvd.
702.733.3333
www.xburlesqueuniversity.com

X Burlesque University is located at the Flamingo and they offer dance classes put on by the sexy girls of X Burlesque. These gals are hot as fire and will teach you a lot of their stage moves in a seventy-five-minute class. If you've seen their show then you'll want to learn how to move, dance, and tease your audience like them. They even give you makeup tips so you'll wow your lover with that exotic burlesque look.

LAS VEGAS BURLESQUE CLASSES
1800 Industrial Rd. #205
702.625.0495
www.lasvegasburlesqueclasses.com

They offer hour-long burlesque party classes in the art of the striptease, where you'll learn how to work a feather boa like a pro. Plus they offer drop-in classes for those last-minute out-of-towners. Or attend one of their monthly burlesque workshops, where you can learn to twirl your tassels, how to make pasties, and much more. If you're interested in becoming a professional burlesque performer, they offer intensive stage-performance courses. More juicy details are available on their website.

AERIAL CLASSES

TRAPEZE LAS VEGAS
121 E. Sunset Blvd.
702.551.4858
www.trapezelasvegas.com

Located in the Sport Center of Las Vegas, Trapeze Las Vegas is just that—a professional trapeze class put on by professional circus performers. If you want to fly through the air and attempt a catch high above the ground (with a net below you, so don't worry), they can help you live out this fantasy and face your fear. They also teach silk classes, which start on the ground with basic wraps and work up to aerial techniques, hand balancing for excellent upper body strength, and even trampoline skills.

SHINE ALTERNATIVE FITNESS
6415 S. Tenaya Way, Suite 100
702.420.2358
www.shinealternativefitness.com

Alternative Fitness isn't just about getting a great body, it's about feeling confident and beautiful in oneself. They offer aerial classes with silk hammocks and a mix of yoga poses, and you can also take Zumba, pole fitness, cardio-boxing, and dance classes. Their fitness classes emphasize embracing natural movements and stimulating your whole body.

TANGO CLASSES

TANGO WITH JUDY
Broadway Hall
3375 S. Decatur Blvd.
www.tangowithjudy.com

Join Judy every Tuesday and Thursday at Broadway Hall for levels one, two and three tango classes. She even offers private sessions, practice dance classes on Tuesdays for only $6 and a Cabaret Theater Tango Show that students can take part in by signing up.

SALSA CLASSES

DANCE CHARISMA
3650 S. Jones Blvd. #16
702.364.8700
www.dancecharisma.com

Dance Charisma has been in business since 1992, so you can expect quality instruction from them. They offer a free class on Monday nights for new-comers! They have group classes as well, and offer a wide variety of dance styles. They break down the many styles into "Social Dances," "Rhythm & Latin," and "Smooth & Standard." Some of the sexier styles they teach are Bolero, Night Club Two Step, and Tango.

SIN CITY SALSEROS
702.301.1091
www.sincitysalseros.net

They have been around almost as long as Dance Charisma, and are working hard to become Las Vegas' #1 salsa dance troupe. Sin City Salseros have great rates and are full of hot young dancers, so check them out if you're after hot new moves. They also dance all over the city, so you can join them at exotic clubs and great restaurants and practice your moves outside of the studio.

ARTHUR MURRAY LAS VEGAS
4550 S. Maryland Pkwy., Suite N
702.798.4552
4440 S. Durango Dr., Suite A
702.876.3131
www.arthurmurraylasvegas.com

This is, of course, a legendary school that offers many dance styles. They've been in the Las Vegas area since 1981, and their salsa classes are top-notch. They participate in medal programs that can qualify you for high-level dance competitions such as "Superama," which is the highest competition among Arthur Murray dance studios. It's held in Las Vegas every October and brings in wonderful dancers from around the world. Don't let the competitions intimidate you. If you just want to learn a nice ballroom dance for your wedding, you can do that, too.

BELLY DANCING CLASSES

BAREFOOT SANCTUARY
6689 S. Las Vegas Blvd.
702.821.5017
www.barefootsanctuary.com

You can learn different types of belly dancing, along with how to use finger cymbals (zills) and veils in your routine. Plus they offer various workshop classes such as "Emotional Freedom Through The Hips" where you'll learn about the functions and anatomy of the hips, how to tune into what your hips are telling you and more. They also offer yoga and meditation classes, including a sacred fire dance.

AMIRA
www.amirasbelly.com

Amira is a world-class instructor who teaches not only at the Las Vegas Athletic Club, but also privately and online. You can get lessons from her and not have to leave your house or hotel room! She also can be booked for private events and hosts yoga and belly dancing cruises and vacations. Another amazing talent of hers is making custom silk veils. Everything she sells is either made by her or endorsed by her. They are 100% silk, gorgeous, and reasonably priced.

ARADIA
8665 W. Flamingo Rd. #110
702.808.3430
www.aradialv.com

Aradia is an excellent instructor and can get you moving in all the right ways. She offers beginner and intermediate-level classes at the Las Vegas School of Dance on Tuesday nights. She performs all over town, as well as in the annual Las Vegas Belly Dance Intensive (www.bellydanceintensive.com).

RAKS ESTELA
702.575.3744
www.raksestela.com

Raks Estela teaches in her home studio and offers special "girl party" packages. She has a private MeetUp group (www.meetup.com/bellyclass) that you can join to find all the latest information on her group classes and available times for private lessons. She can also teach classes in Spanish. Grab your girlfriends and head out for a night of belly dance lessons with the lovely Raks Estela. You won't regret it.

THE ROCKY MOUNTAIN BELLY DANCE COMPANY
702.825.1971
www.rmbdc.org

This place offers a nice service: "Bellygrams." You can hire a belly dancer to deliver a fun and sexy belly dance to someone. The dances are about fifteen minutes long and the price varies on how far they have to travel to deliver the dance. They also offer private and group instruction and can be hired to dance at your party or event.

HULA CLASSES

LAS VEGAS HULA
1913 Green Pkwy., Suite D, Henderson
702.401.0656
www.lasvegashula.com

Las Vegas Hula offers hula classes and other really cool Polynesian dances you may not have heard of before. They perform in events across the city and students are encouraged to participate in them. They also teach yoga, Pilates, and even Hindi dances at their school.

HOT HULA FITNESS
www.hothulafitness.com

Try out this really interesting and sexy class, Hot Hula Fitness, that offers a total body workout in sixty minutes. It really works your core, so come ready for some tummy punishment. As their website states: "Inspired by the dances of the Pacific Islands, Hot Hula fitness incorporates easy-to-perform dance movements set to the sounds of traditional Polynesian drum beats fused with funky music." They offer classes in gyms and studios all over Las Vegas, so visit their website for locations and schedules.

SKIN CITY

HOST A NAUGHTY PARTY

A lot of people come to Las Vegas for one reason—to party. Unless you're a local, you're most likely to get crazy in Sin City. The city caters to those seeking a party they'll never forget, something legendary that will be bragged or whispered about for years to come. If you're in charge of this party, there are many ways to do it right. Las Vegas will help you make it as decadent, bizarre, and freaky as you want. I have a lot of great ideas to make your bachelorette party, girls' night out extravaganza, or night of birthday debauchery unforgettable. Of course, you don't need a birthday, anniversary, or impending wedding to throw a naughty party. You can plan a special night for you and your lover that might involve hiring an exotic dancer to come to your hotel room. Or maybe you want to impress a new batch of clients for work. Keep reading for ways to turn your party into a naughty time.

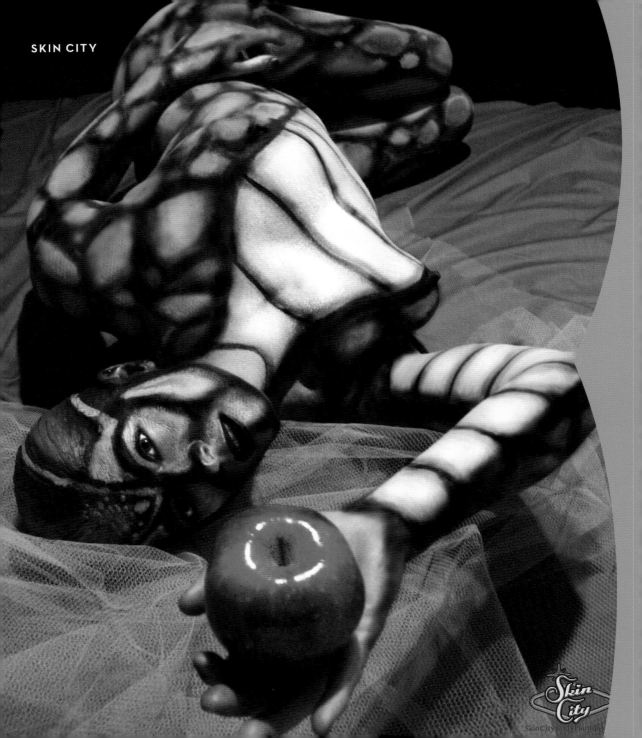

NAUGHTY FOOD

NAKED SUSHI ENTERTAINMENT
949.566.5627
www.nakedsushientertainment.com

You'll want food, so why not have it served on a naked woman? Naked Sushi Entertainment can provide you with a gorgeous Asian model naked on a table and covered in top-rate sushi. They will cater your event and can also provide body painting services, D.J.s, and lingerie hostesses.

BODY PAINT

SKIN CITY BODY PAINTING
1209 South Main St.
702.431.7546
www.skincitybodypainting.com

Want to add a little naughtiness to your party? Or maybe you want to wear body paint out on the town to an event? They can get a painted model to greet your guests and pose for pictures, or they can paint sexy and fun artwork on your guests (or both!). They also do temporary tattoos, henna body art, and more.

SHOWGIRLS

LAS VEGAS SHOWGIRLS
702.939.0653
www.showgirlsinlasvegas.com

Want classic Las Vegas showgirls to greet your guests? You can even have them pose for photographs and help assist with champagne service. They are also available for full production theatre or cabaret shows. Plus they have over twenty sexy showgirl costumes with lots of feathers, rhinestones, and sparkles to impress your guests. They also have celebrity impersonators who can work your party.

REAL VEGAS SHOWGIRLS
702.401.4815
www.realvegasshowgirls.com

This showgirl service has top-notch showgirls who have worked parties at the Playboy mansion. They claim to have *true* showgirls and proof that they're the real deal. They also offer show*boys*, as well as cancan dancers, boxer girls, Santa's helpers, sexy dealers, and an Elvis! Plus you can visit their website to pick out which costumes you'd like your showgirls to wear to match the theme of your event.

PREMIER SHOWGIRLS
5625 Arville Street, Suite E
702.243.9000 ext. 23
www.premiershowgirls.com

This is another great showgirl service. They'll go anywhere in North America to work your party! They've worked a lot of high-profile events, so you can be sure you'll get great quality from them. Their "Living Libations" costumes are astounding! Imagine a beautiful woman in a dress decorated with glasses of champagne or other cocktails. You can walk up, take off part of her dress, and drink it!

SEXY ENTERTAINMENT

LAS VEGAS ACRO ENTERTAINMENT PRODUCTION
702.241.2432
www.LVAEP.com
www.duojoys.com

You'll need entertainment for your party, and Las Vegas offers plenty of it. Flexuality is the sexy balancing act of Tom and Magda. They make art with their bodies and you'll be amazed at what they can do. Be sure to ask about the Flexuality show with Magda and Alyssa. Two lovely women in lingerie wrapping themselves around each other? What's not to like?

TWIST IT UP
2451 North Rainbow Boulevard, Unit 2041
702.461.7192
www.twistitup.org

Twist It Up offers contortionists and full circus performance themes—everything from stilt walkers to plate spinners. If you want tarot card readers to intrigue your guests, hula-hoop spinners to mesmerize them, or even a "girl in a bubble," they can bring it to you.

AERIAL ARTISTRY
917.755.7744
www.aerialartistry.com

This isn't just a service to hire aerial dancers. They can bring you silk dancers, acrobats, drag performers, magicians, and more. One of their specialties is the "Champagne Chandelier." Imagine a lovely performer hanging upside-down and doing a breath-taking performance inside a chandelier decorated with flutes of champagne, which they pour for you during the act!

24 SEVEN PRODUCTIONS
3120 West Post Rd.
702.731.2470
www.24sevenpro.com

If you want a full entertainment company to organize the party for you, you can't do much better than 24 Seven Productions. They have over fifty years of party-planning and event-coordinating experience. They can bring you

D.J.s, dancers, and even holographic effects for your party. You can even rent furniture from them if you need it. They have exclusive bands that work for them to cover every music taste, like the lovely 1940s-themed Swing City Dolls or the naughty-looking rock band Jaggedy Ann.

DANCERS

VICTORIA
702.415.3561
www.dancebyvictoria.com

Don't forget dancers! Victoria is a professional belly dancer who does solo performances (and even "Bellygrams!") and also teaches the art if you're interested. Her performances mix traditional Egyptian music with modern pop. She encourages guest participation at the end, and who wouldn't want to strut their stuff with her?

LAS VEGAS HULA
702.401.0656
www.lasvegashula.com

This top-notch hula dance service can provide hula performers and fire dancers. You can book shows lasting thirty minutes to two hours. The basic package includes three hula girls, two hunky warriors, and an emcee. The deluxe "Polynesian Package" includes lei greeters, six dancers, an emcee, live drumming, and even a fire knife dancer.

LAS VEGAS BURLESQUE CLASSES

1800 Industrial Road, #205
702.625.0495
www.lasvegasburlesqueclasses.com

These lovely ladies will not only teach you the art of burlesque, they can provide dancers for your party. Their burlesque parties are great for a bachelorette party, birthday party, or even just a girls' night out. They even provide the feather boas and elbow-length gloves.

SEX TOY PARTY

PARTY GALS
800.621.4181
www.partygals.biz

If you want to keep the sexy theme going, you could always contact a Party Gals consultant to host a sex toy party. You can call their 1-800 number to find a coach in the Las Vegas area and set up your naughty party for any occasion: girls' night out; afternoon dirty tea; or a slumber, bachelorette, divorce, or couples party. The hostess of the party (whoever books the party) will receive 10% of the party, hostess gifts, and a chance to earn a cruise trip.

SEX PARTY
Nikki Lundberg
www.nikkilundberg.com

Nikki Lundberg is a Las Vegas–based sex coach. She teaches a wide variety of subjects, including communication skills for couples, erotic massage, and even courses on anal sex and female ejaculation. You can contact her for her famous "sex and wine" party for a night of fun and kinky learning.

BACHELORETTE PARTY

BACHELORETTE VEGAS
800.920.8847
www.bachelorettevegas.com

If you want to plan a sexy and wild party for your favorite girl (or you), you might want to call these folks. They consider themselves to be the ultimate authority in planning bachelorette parties. They can get you tickets to see Chippendale dancers, limousine service to and from your hotel, VIP entry into some of the hottest nightclubs, pole-dancing lessons, and even a four-course meal in their "Bachelorette All Night" package.

STRIPPERS

RISQUE KITTY
877.618.8826
www.risquekittystrippers.com/las-vegas-strippers.html

They have a lot of lovely ladies and sexy men who will spice up any party. Scroll through their website to see their selection of eye candy and let your imagination run wild. They offer one, two, and three-stripper shows for various prices. They even offer a wild "Girl Wet Dream Show," which involves two hotties "interacting with each other." Yum!

SIN CITY STRIPPERS
702.433.5793
www.sincitystrippers.com

Need a male stripper for your bachelorette party? Check. Need a couple hot girls to spice up your nightclub event? Check. Need a stripper dressed in a hot dog costume? Yes, check. Sin City Strippers not only offers male and female strippers, they offer "mascot" strippers, she-males, oil wrestling, and even more kinky services.

EXOTIC DANCER LAS VEGAS
702.496.8798
www.exoticdancerslasvegas.com

They offer male and female strippers and a wide variety of services like stripper-grams, go-go dancers, sexy Santas and elves, and "Double Trouble" (two male strippers for the price of one!). You can choose different outfits for the men (cop, fireman, doctor, etc.). They even offer topless poker hostesses if you're having gambling at your party. They will come to you and can strip down to just a G-string or completely naked, tease you privately, and entertain everyone with wild party tricks.

POOL SCENE

The Las Vegas pool scene is like nothing I've ever seen before, but then again that's Vegas for you. There are pools, and then there are beach clubs. A Las Vegas beach club is like a daytime nightclub. Anyone can get in as long as they pay a fee. People come to beach clubs to drink, mingle, dance, and look their best. You don't just show up with your beach bag, no makeup, hair in a ponytail, and a wearing a one-piece bikini. You come wearing high heels (Yes, to a pool!), jewelry, your sexiest bikini, hair fixed, makeup on, self-tanner and shimmer on your body, purse, and designer sunglasses. And it's not just the women who come looking their best as the men look just as good as some of the women.

Also, beach clubs bring in the best D.J.s from around the world. So if you're looking for a party in the sun, then head to a beach club. If you're looking for just laying out in the sun, then head to your hotel pool. I've created a list of the pools with some of the best beach clubs in the city. Check out any of these the next time you're choosing where to stay.

THE POND AT GREEN VALLEY RANCH
2300 Paseo Verde Pkwy.
702.617.7744
www.greenvalleyranch.sclv.com/hotel/pool.aspx

This is the most intimate beach club, probably because it's not on the Strip. It never has a cover and you can get bottle service there for just $75.00. How about $25.00 for a pitcher of margaritas on Tuesdays? Cabanas for $100.00? Great drink specials on Saturdays and Sundays? What's not to like?

THE DECK AT ALIANTE STATION
7300 N. Aliante Pkwy., North Las Vegas
702.692.7777
www.aliantegaming.com/enjoy/#pool

This is another intimate pool club outside of the Strip. It has a gorgeous long pool lined with palm trees. It looks like an oasis, which I suppose it is in a way. It's a half-hour drive out of the city, but worth it if you're looking for a more "chillwave" atmosphere for your beach party.

CHERRY POOL AT RED ROCK HOTEL
11011 W. Charleston Blvd.
702.797.7297
www.redrock.sclv.com/hotel/pool.aspx

This is a fantastic pool party off the Strip, but it feels like you're in the middle of the Strip action with gaming by the pool. The entire pool area is huge, with lots of lounges and cabanas, but I like the Cherry Pool best.

It's sexy, intimate, and has lovely cabanas and lounge chairs next to it. It's a nice place for a sexy encounter.

MARQUEE DAYCLUB AT COSMOPOLITAN
3708 S. Las Vegas Blvd.
702.333.9000
www.marqueelasvegas.com

This is a wonderful facility with a wading pool, full pool, nice cabanas, and fantastic views of the Strip. They get a lot of top D.J.s here, and they have a nice stage for seeing live bands. It's one of the newest dayclubs on the Strip, so a lot of sexy people hang out there.

ENCORE BEACH CLUB AT WYNN
3121 S. Las Vegas Blvd.
702.770.7300
www.encorebeachclub.com

This amazing place brings in some of the top D.J.s in the world. They've had Skrillex, Diplo, Deadmau5, Afrojack, and many more there. It's a huge area (60,000 square feet) and has nice private cabanas with their own hot tubs. It also turns into the Surrender nightclub once the sun goes down. If you stay at the Wynn, you get VIP access to Encore.

AZURE AT PALAZZO
3325 S. Las Vegas Blvd.
702.767.3724
www.palazzo.com/azure.html

Located on the third floor of Palazzo, this beach club offers a nice mix of partying and/or chilling out with your friends. It's based on clubs in the French Riviera and has D.J.s spinning house music, but the atmosphere is that of a spa—so feel free to relax. If you want some privacy but to still be near the action, you can rent a daybed.

SAPPHIRE POOL AND DAY CLUB
3025 Industrial Rd.
702.869.0003
www.sapphirepoollv.com

This pool has the lovely advantage of being at a *strip club*. Celebrities and adult film stars frequent here quite often. You can rent daybeds and cabanas and party with some of the hottest exotic dancers in town at their pool parties. They bring in a lot of good D.J.s and even have "Mix It Up" networking events for businesses. They aren't topless but you can wear pasties, which they provide.

SAPPHIRE POOL AND DAY CLUB

TOPLESS POOLS

Another naughty thing about Vegas, is that you can swim and layout topless! Woohoo! You just have to know where to do it. You can't just take your top off at Circus Circus and giggle after you spill your mojito on your boobies. There are places that will kick you out for doing such things, despite the protests of everyone who wants you to stay. You can take the girls for a topless swim at several spots in Las Vegas, and I'm here to tell you where they are.

Topless pools are different from the beach clubs I described because, well, they're topless. The real difference, however, is that they are more low-key, as the adult area is usually smaller. Plus they usually don't have D.J.s spinning loud music, which can be refreshing after hearing it in so many clubs night after night. People are dressed more low-key at topless pools. They're more worried about how their boobies look than wearing a designer bikini, cover up, and heels.

THE VOO AT RIO
3700 W. Flamingo Rd.
702.777.6774
www.riolasvegas.com/casinos/rio/casino-misc/the-voo-detail.html

There are two pools at Rio. One is Voodoo Beach, which has a beach, four pools, and five Jacuzzi spas. The other is The Voo, where you can go topless and avoid tan lines. You can also get a massage poolside. Dare to be decadent, I say. You must be 21 years and older and there's a cover charge for men. Women are free, of course. Plus locals receive 50% off bottle service on Thursdays and Sundays.

MOOREA BEACH CLUB AT MANDALAY BAY
39950 S. Las Vegas Blvd.
702.632.4760
www.mandalaybay.com/beach/moorea-beach-club/

The Moorea Beach Club is an upscale adult club. It costs $10.00 for women and $40 to $50.00 for men to get in there, but it's worth it. They offer private cabanas, excellent views, and wonderful personal service by their attendants (who are usually quite attractive). And if you want, you have access to the Mandalay Bay pool, but you'll have to put your top back on before you do.

VENUS POOL AT CAESARS PALACE
3570 S. Las Vegas Blvd.
702.731.7266
www.venuspoolclub.com

The Venus Pool (in the "Garden of the Gods" pool area) has eleven cabanas, four couches, fourteen day beds and chaise lounge chairs, and some of the best food found at any Las Vegas pool. Ladies are always free, but men have to pay to see our boobies. If you like a European flavor to your poolside lounging, this is the place to go.

NAKED POOL AT ARTISAN
1501 W. Sahara Ave.
702.214.4000
www.artisanhotel.com/poolcabana/

The Naked Pool is a bit of a misnomer. No one is actually naked there, but the swimsuits on the hostesses leave little to the imagination. It's another European-themed pool with delightful private areas and sexy hostesses who serve drinks and food. This place caters more to couples and to those who are looking for a more intimate pool setting. Seating is limited, so call in advance to reserve a day bed or cabana.

THE HIDEOUT AT THE GOLDEN NUGGET
129 Fremont St., Downtown
702.385.7111
www.goldennugget.com/lasvegas/pool_thehideout.asp

The Hideout is an intimate pool area on the third floor of "the Tank," a massive pool area at this off-the-Strip gem of a hotel. They have a two-story infinity pool that you have to see to believe. It's a flat $20.00 rate to get in for guys and gals, but what you get in return is privacy. Also, the H2O Bar there is quite good.

BARE POOL LOUNGE AT THE MIRAGE
3400 S. Las Vegas Blvd.
702.508.5656
www.barepoollv.com

Bare Pool Lounge is a luxurious spot with great VIP service. The surrounding palm trees conveniently screen your boobies from prying eyes outside the pool area. Bare's intimate 14,000 square feet offers six cabanas, eight VIP beds, four tables, and two luxury dipping pools. Make sure to visit their website to view their D.J. lineup and to reserve a spot for "Bare Sundays Brunch," with brunch served all day and an open Bloody Mary bar.

TAO BEACH AT THE VENETIAN
3355 S. Las Vegas Blvd.
702.388.8338
www.taobeach.com

This place is so lavish that they provide a DVD library for private cabanas with flat-screen TVs and DVD players. The bar at Tao Beach is thirty feet long and has great drinks. The cabanas are top-notch and the D.J.s spin quality beats. A lot of celebrities show up here, so look your best and keep your eyes open. Also, *Maxim* hosts an event there on Friday and has open casting for models. However, the pool is only topless during the week, Monday through Thursday, not the weekends. And it's 21 years and older for the topless area.

SUNSET POOL AT THE WYNN
3131 S. Las Vegas Blvd.
702.770.7000
www.wynnlasvegas.com/activities/pools

Sunset Pool is a topless pool for hotel guests only. If you're not staying there, you'll have to find someone who is if you really want to go there. They have nice cabanas with flat-screen TVs and you can lounge in the pool on these cute lily pad floaters. This pool is also open seasonally, so be sure to call ahead to find out if you need to bring your tanning oil.

NAKED IN LAS VEGAS

If you want to walk around naked, Las Vegas is a good place to do it. The weather is usually perfect for going nude (just think twice in the winter, as the nights can get downright chilly in the desert). The city loves skin, so you can find places to embrace the nudist lifestyle if you choose.

Don't forget that nudist events and swinger parties are not the same thing. Even though both groups are proud of and into celebrating their bodies, nudists and swingers usually have different ideas and levels of excitement about being naked. The two groups are not mutually exclusive, there is some overlap (and a possibility for a very kinky Venn diagram). However, by and large, swingers aren't nudists (except for when getting it on), and nudists aren't swingers. There are some nudists who are swingers, but don't assume everyone is. Bottom line: if you go to a nudist event with a swinger mindset, you will probably be disappointed or even asked to leave. So, make sure you understand and follow the rules of any nudist event you attend.

LAS VEGAS BARES

www.lasvegasbares.com

Las Vegas Bares hosts several nudist events throughout the year, including overnight trips to hot springs or nudist resorts in Nevada. Their in-town events are held at members' homes and are great ways to meet fellow nudists and have fun.

THE NUDIST CLUBHOUSE EXPO

www.nudistclubhouse.com

This is one of the biggest nudist events in the country, usually held in early summer. The expo takes over an entire resort and has many exhibitors (and not just the people walking around the pool party!) and guest speakers. They even have private nude mini-golf events! If you want to learn all about the nudist lifestyle, this is a good place to start.

LAS VEGAS NUDISTS

www.lasvegasnudists.com

This is another "non-landed" club (in that they don't have a permanent location for their activities) that caters to couples and hosts many events in the city—including nude Twister and piñata parties!

Naughty Shopping

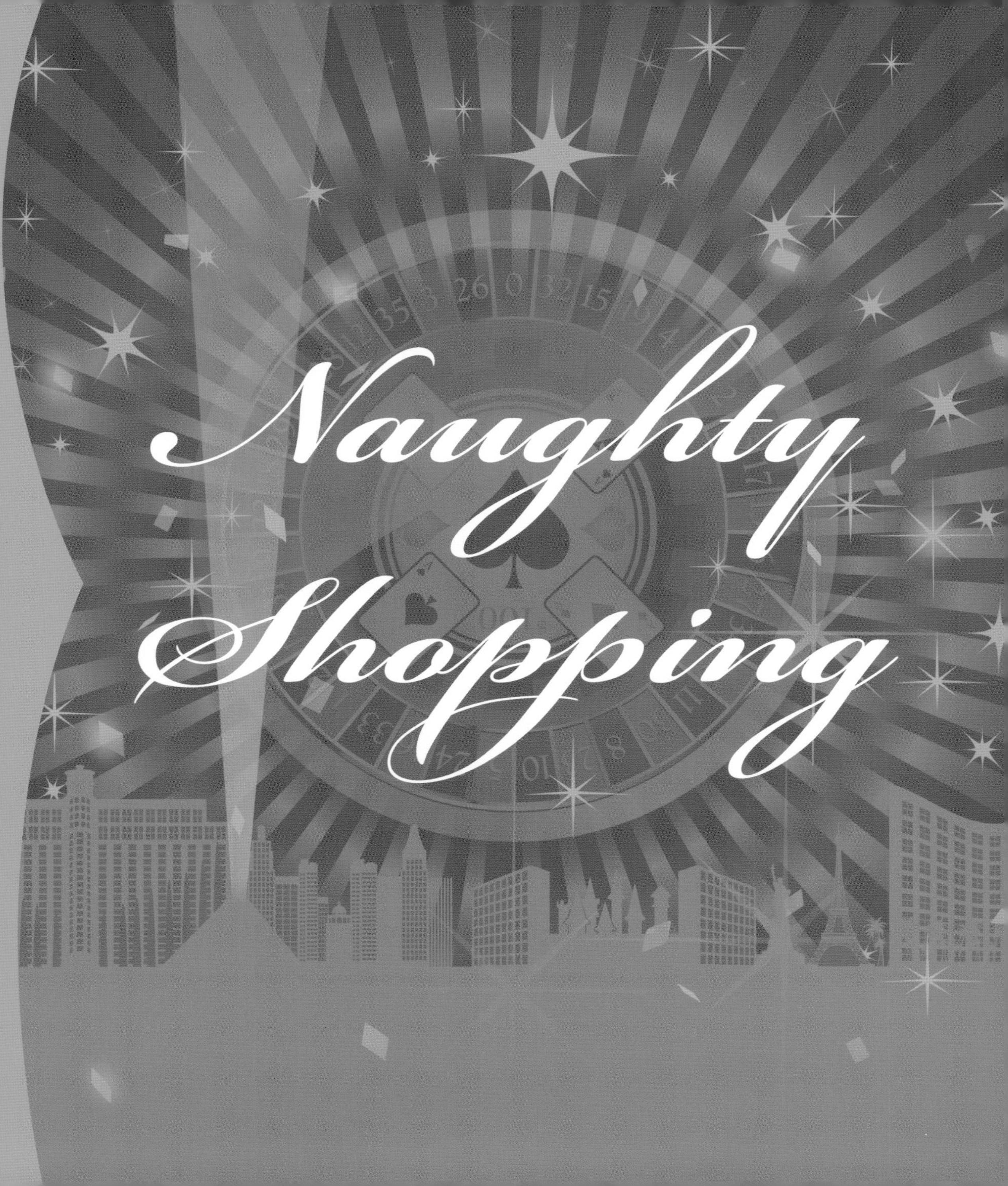

BEAUTY

Las Vegas is full of sexy, lovely people, and you can be one of them. The city provides a lot of places to make you look fabulous for a weekend with your girlfriends, a bachelorette party, a wedding, or just to feel great for anytime of the week. However, Las Vegas can take a big toll on your body and looks, especially if you're staying more than two nights. Here's a list of ways to keep you looking good in Vegas with your clothes on or off.

SEXY HAIR

COLOR SALON AT CAESARS PALACE
3570 Las Vegas Blvd.
702.731.7791
www.michaelboychuck.com

This place is visually stunning with its crystal chandeliers and white, grey, and metallic greys throughout the salon. Besides offering hair extensions, coloring, and highlights, they also offer makeup applications and eyelash extensions where you can get all dolled up for a night out on the town. They offer Makeup & Mimosas Happy Hour everyday from 2 p.m. to 4 p.m., and a D.J. spins on the weekends.

SEXY SMILE

SEXY VEGAS SMILES
2451 Professional Ct., #110
702.240.4242
www.sexyvegassmiles.com

Dr. Suzi Su is a fully licensed dentist who offers the best modern dental treatments for whitening, straightening, and even invisible braces. Don't forget that your smile is often the first thing people notice, so you want to dazzle them. Dr. Su can give you an "In Office Opalescence Boost" to have your smile sparking for your night on the town.

SEXY TAN

ILLUMINATE YOU
702.493.7338
www.illuminateyoumobilespraytan.com

Host a tanning party with your friends and Illuminate You will come to your place anywhere in Las Vegas or Henderson. This package includes a bottle of wine! Or if you just want to look good for a night out on the town, you can buy individual spray tans or monthly packages. They even offer eyelash extensions in synthetic, mink and silk lashes to help bring out your eyes.

SEXY BEAVER

BOX
420 S. Rampart
702.893.9993
www.bikiniwaxing.com

This salon specializes in bikini waxing. Their website puts it best: "We've made getting the hair ripped out of your various body parts by pouring hot wax on them an experience you can't wait to have time & time again." Their "human landscapers" are highly trained and will make sure your waxing is the best experience possible.

SEXY MAKEOVER

YOUR BEAUTY CALL
702.530.1661
www.yourbeautycall.com

Don't have time to make it to a salon? Or are you just having too much fun at your hotel to make the trip? Call *Your Beauty Call* (not Your *Booty* Call, that's an entirely different service). These two sexy stylists will come to your hotel and get you glamorous for your wedding, party, or date with your lover.

SEXY ANUS

WAX LAS VEGAS
9809 W. Flamingo Rd.
702.221.4929
www.waxlasvegas.com

They offer a wide variety of waxing services at good prices. They do anal waxing and bleaching for men and women. You can even "bling your thing" with a crystal tattoo. They'll make sure your lady parts look good. As their website says, "Waxed Beavers Get More Wood!"

SEXY FITNESS

THE PILATES MISTRESS
702.608.2673
www.pilatesmistress.com

Tracy, the Pilates mistress, isn't really a dominatrix, but she will whip your booty into shape with her intensive Pilates workouts. She's a certified trainer, gorgeous, and will make you sweat. She believes in regular practice in order to reap the benefits of Pilates, and will help you discover muscles you didn't know you had.

LAS VEGAS NAKED YOGA
3275 Industrial Rd.
702.369.6442
www.lasvegasnakedyoga.com

Located in different locations around town, Las Vegas Naked Yoga is a great place to work out. If you enjoy doing yoga or want to learn more about it, why not do it while you're naked? Clothing can be restrictive for some poses, so naked yoga can be quite liberating and take your practice to a level you haven't experienced. They have men's and co-ed classes, and you don't have to worry about it being a "hook-up" atmosphere. All the instructors are professional and certified in many styles of yoga and Pilates. They stress celebrating and discovering your body, not peep shows.

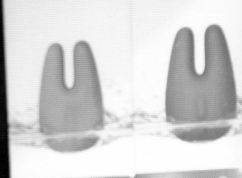

FORM 2

FORM 2

NAUGHTY STORES

Images of lingerie are all over Las Vegas, as are lingerie stores. Whether you visit a strip club, brothel, a showgirls show, nightclub, bar, or Vegas hotel, you're sure to see someone in lingerie (and sometimes not much, if anything, else).

Lingerie is part of Vegas culture. From the first brothels here on Block 16 in downtown, to the showgirls, burlesque performers, strippers, and go-go dancers, sexy lingerie has been part of the fabric (pun intended) of the city. Sex sells, and lingerie helps push the product.

What other city would host one of the biggest lingerie tradeshows? Vegas of course! The International Lingerie Show comes every year to Vegas to display some of the sexiest lingerie in the world.

Nothing feels and looks sexier on a woman (besides her naked body) than lingerie. What better way to feel sexy on a night out than wearing something sexy under your dress? Or surprise your lover by buying something sexy to show off when the two of you get back to your hotel room.

LINGERIE STORES

AGENT PROVOCATEUR AT CAESARS PALACE
3500 Las Vegas Blvd.
702.696.7174
www.agentprovocateur.com

What I love about this place is the variety of styles they have for you. Need a smoking hot bikini for that pool party? They have it. Need a sexy black teddy that will make your lover drop his drink? They have that, too. They offer some great collections. The Bridal collection is lovely, the Soiree collection is especially luxurious, and the Classics collection never goes out of style. Their "Luxe Luggage" is also fantastic for your next naughty holiday.

LA PERLA AT CAESARS PALACE
3500 Las Vegas Blvd.
702.732.9820
www.laperla.com

This lovely high-end lingerie store has some of the best bras available and some wild lingerie fashions. It's located close to the casino in Caesars Palace, so it's a great place to treat yourself after winning big at the tables. Their collections are outstanding! They sell a wide variety of sexy items, including basics, bridal, perfume, swimwear, and men's underwear.

VICTORIA'S SECRET AT CAESARS PALACE
3500 Las Vegas Blvd.
702.893.0903
www.victoriassecret.com

You can always count on Victoria's Secret for sexy items and reasonable prices. If Agent Provocateur and La Perla are out of your price range, you can still treat yourself at Victoria's Secret to some sexy pajamas, bras, panties, and garters. You don't have to spend a lot of money to look and feel sexy.

FREDERICK'S OF HOLLYWOOD
Three locations: 4300 Meadows Lane/702.870.8129
3680 South Maryland Pkwy./702.735.5065
3200 Las Vegas Blvd./702.893.9001
www.fredericks.com

They're not just in L.A.! There are three locations to serve you in Las Vegas, so you're never too far away to get some naughty lingerie. Their "Ultra Sexy" line is just that, and sure to wow your lover with their fetish-themed lingerie. The Harriet Collection is full of silky sexy stuff (not to mention Swarovski crystals) like classic robes, dresses, and bras. Their Hollywood Dream Corset line is simple, elegant, and naughty all at the same time.

GO SEXY AT FLAMINGO
3555 S. Las Vegas Blvd.
702.733.3111
www.flamingolasvegas.com/things-to-do/shopping.html

It's hard to miss this store. Just look for the place with a giant woman's stocking-clad legs framing the entrance to the store. Whether you're naughty or nice, this store has lots of naughty items to spice up your sex life. They sell lingerie, and a lot of it is edible. Need a chocolate thong? Of course you do. Who doesn't? Plus they sell hosiery, bridal and bachelorette gifts, novelties, couple's games, and books.

LOVE JONES AT HARD ROCK
4455 Paradise Rd.
702.693.5000
www.hardrockhotel.com/las-vegas-stores/lingerie

Love Jones "is dedicated to the concept of seduction, sensuality, and the power of the female form." They sell designer lingerie from Elle Macpherson, Blush, and other brands, but they also have exclusive designs you can't get anywhere else. You can also pick up a paddle or whip to go with your sexy outfit. You never know who you'll meet while in Vegas so always be prepared!

KIKI DE MONTPARNASSE AT MGM
3720 S. Las Vegas Blvd.
702.736.7883
www.kikidm.com

This stunning place looks like your fantasy boudoir! You'll want to stay and play all day, especially when you see their bedroom area. They not only sell high-end lingerie, but also exclusive jewelry, naughty home décor, sexy artwork, bath and body items, instruments of pleasure, and items to live out your *Fifty Shades of Grey* fantasies. They have a couple's dressing room so you and your lover can try on intimate wear together. You can go to their photo booth afterwards for some sexy souvenir photos.

BARE ESSENTIALS
4029 W. Sahara Ave.
702.247.4711
www.bareessentialsvegas.com

This store isn't difficult to find. It's next to the 45-foot-tall Statue of Liberty a few minutes off the Strip. They are the exclusive West Coast outlet for designs by Exclusive Costumes and have a wide variety of corsets, stockings, shoes, and costumes. They even sell men's thongs, erotic underwear, shirts, costumes, and more. Take your lover with you to find sexy costumes so you can play dress-up back in your hotel room. And don't forget to pick up a sex toy of your choice to go along with your fantasy play, as they have a full line of erotic sex toys.

SEX-TOY STORES

ADAM & EVE
3231 N. Decatur Blvd.
702.478.6969
www.adamevelasvegas.com

Adam and Eve stores have clearly set a standard in the world of Specialty Retail. While many of their products are adult in nature, one can also find many specialty and novelty gifts lining their racks. This type of atmosphere provides women, men and couples alike with a degree of comfortability and friendliness while shopping for sensual and romantic gifts. With high-quality sex toys, games and other erotica, one may also find lingerie, women and men's apparel, lotions, DVDs and books. This is the perfect place to explore with your better half, or for finding that special gift for a bachelor or bachelorette party.

DÉJÀ VU LOVE BOUTIQUE
Three locations: 4335 West Tropicana Ave./702.367.8002
3247 Industrial Rd./702.894.4167
1514 S. Western Ave./702.308.4605
www.loveboutiqueonline.com

Déjà Vu Love Boutique claims that their store brings couples closer. And I can see why with their array of naughty items available. If you need to pick up a sexy maid costume, a dildo, some lube, and a cock ring in one trip, you can do it at any of their three stores. Plus this is a great place to visit after you're out on the town and looking to get naughty with a lover as they are open late.

LION'S DEN
2923 S. Industrial Rd.
702.892.9315
www.lionsden.com

The Lion's Den started 41 years ago as one of the first adult retail stores in the country and has blossomed into a full retail chain offering high-quality adult toys, gifts and novelties. This new location in Las Vegas has over five thousand square feet of retail space and the biggest video arcade in the city. The Lion's Den seeks to create a safe and comfortable atmosphere that is designed to help bring couples together and enhance the intimacy of their relationships, furthering their sexual exploration and helping to make the sex lives of their dreams come true.

ADULT SUPERSTORE
Four locations: 3850 W. Tropicana Ave./702.798.0144
3226 Spring Mountain Rd./702.247.1101
601 S. Main St./702.383.0601
1147 S. Las Vegas Blvd./702.383.8326
www.vegasadultsuperstore.com

The Adult Superstores sell everything from vibrators to feather boas. The "Giant Mega-Superstore" on West Tropicana and the "Downtown" store on South Main have, among other things, *twin-screen* movie theatres. All the stores offer just about anything you can imagine in terms of sex toys, fetish items, and XXX movies. If you're not sure what to get, they offer many kits that include lubes, dildos, anal beads, and other combinations of fun things for the bedroom.

HUSTLER HOLLYWOOD
6007 Dean Martin Dr.
702.685.6969
www.hustlerhollywood.com

They have everything you want for a wild and sexy night. It's an upscale, multi-level store with a huge selection of sex toys, costumes, lingerie, and more. Plus Larry Flynt's Hustler Club is located right next door! So if you're looking for some eye candy with your lover, head to the strip club for some action. Then after you're both worked up sexually, head to the store to buy your naughty goods and then back to your hotel room for some one-on-one time.

THE LOVE STORE
2100 S. Rainbow Blvd.
702.641.LOVE
www.thelovestore.com

This flagship store location boasts over twelve thousand feet of heavenly, adult retail space in a clean and spacious atmosphere. They offer a naughty selection of toys, clothing, DVDs and books. The Love Store also has the ability to help you put together a themed party for any event you may be having. A knowledgeable and friendly staff is on hand to assist you in any capacity and find you the exact products that you need.

FETISH STORES

THE BLACK ROOM
1000 E. Sahara Ave., Suite 100
702.685.8688
www.theblackroomlasvegas.com

This place imports German fetish fashions, including PVC, metal pieces, leather, and latex. Plus they carry a ton of hot items, including corsets, lingerie, hosiery, electric play, floggers, paddles, restraints, medical play, club wear, and plus-size clothing. They also have a nice selection of menswear. And, if you're really feeling frisky, you should treat yourself to a C-string (which covers even less than a G-string).

THE STUDIO - A FETISH BOUTIQUE
1509 W. Oakey Blvd.
702.214.2851
www.peselectro.com

The Studio is a fetish boutique that specializes in electro-stimulation equipment and all sorts of fetish gear. If you're tired of bondage and spanking and want to take your *Fifty Shades of Grey* to the next level, then add some electrodes to spice things up. They have naughty items for both men and women. Want to keep your man in line? Maybe he needs an electric cock ring. He'll never forget to open the door or pull your chair out again!

LADY C LEATHER
4037 W. Sahara Ave.
702.641.3834
www.ladycleather.com

A kinky shop that's located off the beaten path, Lady C Leather has a lot of lovely fetish gear and handcrafted fetish toys. Plus the lovely Lady C herself is ready to help you. Need to find the local rope bondage group? Just ask Lady C as she's helping you try on that corset.

SHOWGIRL COSTUME STORES

SHOW-OFF! LAS VEGAS COSTUMES
6400 S. Eastern Ave.
702.739.6995
www.showofflasvegas.com

This store provides costumes for production companies, pageants, and resorts, so their quality is high. No two costumes are alike (unless you want them to be), because everything is handcrafted. If your lover has a showgirl fetish (and don't all of us, at least a little bit?), you can get a great costume here complete with feathered headdress if you want. Head over and check out their stunning pieces. They also rent nearly any kind of costume you can imagine.

SAJEELA DESIGN
702.416.0470
www.sajeeladesign.com

Sajeela is an amazing designer of showgirl and burlesque costumes, and her work with feathers is nothing short of fantastic. Her feather fans are works of art, and her peacock feather pasties are delightful. She even decorates high heels with these feathers. Want to play super villain? Check out her Poison Ivy dress. You can be the sexy villain and your boy toy can be Batman (or your girlfriend could be Batgirl!).

PARADISE COSTUMES
551 E. Oakley Blvd.
702.361.6121
www.paradisecostumes.com

They have been in business since the 1970s. They provided costumes for Hollywood before moving to Las Vegas, so their stuff has a lot of glamour. Their ostrich-feather headdresses are amazing. They have costumes that can make you look like you stepped out of an Olivia painting. They also have other costumes, like wizard robes and angel wings for other fun fantasies you may want to try while you're in Sin City. And why not dress up your lover in something naughty. Have a Roman soldier fantasy? Then check out their sexy costumes for men.

RAINBOW FEATHER CO.
1036 S. Main St.
702.598.0988
www.rainbowfeatherco.com

This is the perfect location to find feathers for your showgirl costume, bachelorette party, or when taking a strip class in this book. Perhaps you just want to spice things up in the bedroom with your lover by adding the pizazz of costumery or a beautiful, sexy-colored boa. Rainbow Feather Co. is able to get just about any kind of feather and color that your heart desires. They also refurbish fans and costumes and transcend the world of colored feathers to a new and extreme form of Art.

PINUP STORES

BAD ATTITUDE BOUTIQUE
953 E. Sahara Ave. #B-10
702.646.9669
www.badattitude.com

They have lovely corsets (including fetish corsets available in lambskin leather) and bustier tops so that you can dress up as your favorite pinup. They even have costume corsets, such as Christmas and military themes, so you can act out your pinup fantasies. Their website only offers a few styles, so make sure to stop by their store for a bigger selection.

BETTIE PAGE CLOTHING
Two locations: 3663 S. Las Vegas Blvd./702.636.1100
3500 S. Las Vegas Blvd./702.369.8277
www.bettiepageapparel.com

They have two locations: The Forum Shops at Caesars Palace and The Shops at Miracle Mile. Sexy, fun, and retro, Bettie Page Clothing stores can make you feel like you're in an episode of "Mad Men" or are a Hollywood pinup star. The prices are affordable and they have a big selection of gorgeous dresses, separates, and a fun assortment of accessories. If you want a sexy dress that's different from all the other girls in Vegas, then visit this store as you'll definitely stand out in the crowd.

NAUGHTY TREATS

Everyone has a sweet tooth, and Las Vegas has plenty of ways to satisfy it. I'm not talking about hiring an escort (not yet, at least). I'm talking about chocolates, cakes, candies, and other goodies. Need a naughty cake for your birthday or bachelorette party? Never fear, naughty Vegas bakers will come to your rescue. Want some luscious chocolates to put on your lover's pillow (or to eat off him or her!)? Las Vegas has world-class chocolatiers. Besides, dark chocolate increases your libido and is actually healthy for your heart in reasonable doses. And if you want lollipops, or ones shaped like nice cocks, you can find those, too.

SEXY CAKES

THE GOURMET CAKE FACTORY
1280 S. Jones Blvd.
702.364.2253
www.tgcf.com

This cake specialist can handle any cake request you may have. They pride themselves on cakes that are not only delicious, but also beautiful. You might not want to eat one of these tasty art pieces. Or maybe you will, especially some of their naughty cakes that leave nothing to the imagination (and their hard-cock cupcakes are fun).

EROTIC BAKERY CAKES
4200 Spring Mountain Rd.
866.396.8429
www.eroticbakeryusa.com

Need a naughty cake in a hurry? These folks need only an hour's notice! They can get you a "he-man torso with king-size dick" cake if you forgot to order one for your friend's bachelorette party. They also have sugar-free and cholesterol-free treats if you need to watch what you eat (and you'll get an eyeful of that he-man cake, that's for sure). You can call at any time, day or night, to order a cake.

FREED'S BAKERY
9815 South Eastern Ave.
702.456.7762
www.freedsbakery.com

Head over to Freed's Bakery and you'll find a bakery that's been in business for over fifty years. They have been featured on *$40 a Day with Rachel Ray* and in *Martha Stewart: Weddings* magazine. They make wonderful bachelorette party cakes, too. The "Playboy Club" cake is a nice one that isn't too bawdy if you want a classy cake. Of course, you can always get one with a giant cock on it, too.

NAUGHTY CAKES
702.401.8981
www.lasvegasnaughtycakes.com

The name says it all. Need cupcakes that look like boobies? How about a cake designed to look like a woman masturbating? Are you on the search for a pole dancer cake, or a cake depicting Santa Claus getting a blowjob? Juliette will get you whatever you need. A lot of her cakes have to be seen (and eaten) to be believed. So visit their website for photos of their naughty cakes.

SEXY CANDIES

SUGAR FACTORY
Four Locations: 3400 S. Las Vegas Blvd./702.565.4767
3500 S. Las Vegas Blvd./702.866.0777
3799 S. Las Vegas Blvd./702.675.4100
3655 S. Las Vegas Blvd./702.331.5511
www.sugarfactorylv.com

The Sugar Factory has four locations to tantalize you. You can find them at the Mirage, Planet Hollywood, the MGM, and Paris (which is their flagship store). Check out their "Violent Lips" temporary lip tattoos. They have lip tattoos in different styles like Gay Pride Rainbow, polka dots, and red glitter. They also have candy underwear your lover can eat off you. This is a great place for fun bachelorette party gifts. All the locations have a huge selection of candies, and you can get your own "couture pop" at any of them. It's a custom-handled lollipop made to your specifications. You can coordinate it with the outfit you're wearing that night!

LICK
Two Locations: 3950 S. Las Vegas Blvd./702.207.4881
3770 S. Las Vegas Blvd./702.730.7777

Lick has two locations: Monte Carlo Resort & Casino and Mandalay Bay. They have sexy photos of lips and tongues hanging on the walls, and they even have a photo booth where you can take pictures of yourself doing naughty things with your tongue and then have them emailed to you. The store will even display your photo on their big screen over the register, which might be an interesting way to find a date! Pretty much everything in this store is naughty, even their T-shirts. They sell penis-shaped suckers, candy g-strings, gummy handcuffs, and even panties! It's full of great treats for a bachelorette party or naughty girls' getaway.

EROTIC ART

It's everywhere! It really is if you step back and take a look around. There are statues of topless women all over Caesars Palace. Women dance in the windows of the Cosmopolitan like living erotic paintings. The water fountain show at the Bellagio looks like a massive cum shot.

So why not take some naughty art home with you to remind you of your trip to Las Vegas? No, you can't take home that sexy Japanese dancer in the schoolgirl outfit you found in the Cosmopolitan window (or maybe you can, depending on your luck and how well you flirt), but you can find a lot of erotic art for your home. Having an erotic art piece in your home can make you feel naughty and get you in the mood. If you're worried about your kids or family seeing it, just don't hang up anything featuring nudity. All that matters is that it turns you on when you look at it. It can be something as sexy as a girl dressed in lingerie or a man and a woman locked in a seductive kiss.

SIN CITY GALLERY
107 E. Charleston Blvd. #100
702.608.2461
www.sincitygallery.com
www.12ofsin.com

This gallery is open Wednesday through Friday and features some amazing exhibitions of erotic art and photography. It also displays erotic sculptures on occasion. Check out the *12" of Sin* juried exhibition if you can. It displays a lot of new art by upcoming artists.

DR. SKETCHY'S ANTI-ART SCHOOL
1025 South First St.
702.489.6339
www.drsketchy.com/lasvegasdrsketchys.blogspot.com
www.lasvegasdrsketchys.blogspot.com

This combines booze, boobies, and Bristol boards to make a fun art event. Dr. Sketchy's Anti-Art School brings lovely fetish, burlesque, and kink performers together with artists of all skill levels. You're encouraged to draw the models however you like. They pose on stage and you can polish your penciling while having a few cocktails, listening to good music, and talking with hot performers and other people who appreciate kinky art. It's held the third Thursday of every month at The Artifice.

NUDE OIL PAINTINGS & BOUDOIR PORTRAITS
5315 N. El Capitan Way
702.236.3818
www.lvstudioart.com

Artist Carol Mittwede is deeply passionate about creating nude oil paintings that reflect the sensual essence found within. Through her bold, dramatic and well-textured strokes, Carol is able to find and convey this essence that sometimes standard boudoir photography is unable to define. Carol is a consummate and professional fine artist. Spending time with her in the studio is comfortable and relaxing, as she invites you to see her work and explore the exact kind of composition that is right for you. A sensual nude portrait is the perfect gift for your lover! Commission oil paintings can also be created from your photos.

A.D. COOK - FIGURATIVE ARTIST
702.875.5676
www.adcfa.com

Magnificent figurative artist A.D. Cook creates impeccable visions of classic, yet contemporary design. His personal mission is to celebrate the timelessness and beauty of the female form through art. Creating sensual, large-scale nudes on canvas or metal, his creations are designed to honor the grace, beauty and complexity of the female spirit. A.D. does perform services on commission and if you are interested in creating a piece, either from a photograph or by modeling yourself, these options are possible.

Check out his site and see what kind of wild, seductive candy for the eyes that this impeccable craftsman has to offer.

NUDE MASTERPIECE LAS VEGAS
www.nudemasterpiece.com

Nude Masterpiece offers itself as an alternative to the more standard fare, boudoir photography found in Vegas. You can either buy their naughty artwork online or book a session with them. While a session with Nude Masterpiece can incorporate elements of boudoir photography, it is the emphasis on Fine Art that truly sets them apart. Working in color, black and white or monochrome, each piece displays the dazzling power of chiaroscuro, sharp lines and an intimate detail to tone. Even more compelling is that a session with Nude Masterpiece is not only a photo shoot, but a total experience for you to be pampered with champagne and chocolates. Gallery and Studio opening soon.

VEGAS RETRO
848 N. Rainbow Blvd. #4185
702.870.8653
www.vegasretro.com

Bringing back the Vegas of old, the Vegas of Sinatra, Sammy and Showgirls galore, Vegas Retro is a site dedicated to the work of celebrated and influential photographer Robert Scott Hooper. Every one of these iconic images is from his vast collection, most of which have gone unpublished. For the first time these images are available in high-quality prints to own. A massive selection spanning three decades of work can be perused through, as you take this historical odyssey through Las Vegas. The work showcases the entertainers, showgirls, burlesque stars, live productions and magazine covers that Hooper had a hand in documenting and creating. Check out Vegas Retro and own a piece of Sin City history!

LENS MASTERS LAS VEGAS
www.meetup.com/lensmasterslv/

Lens Masters of Las Vegas is an online forum that is dedicated to furthering the photographic skill sets of its members through social networking, seminars and training. This group is a must for the budding or amateur photographer seeking to find like minds and build a foundation for working professionally or as an enthusiast. Lens Masters is a great place to meet models, other photographers or others who may be interested in hiring your services! This is a great site if you are just getting into erotic photography and are looking to find models or have your own image captured in all of its naughty splendor!

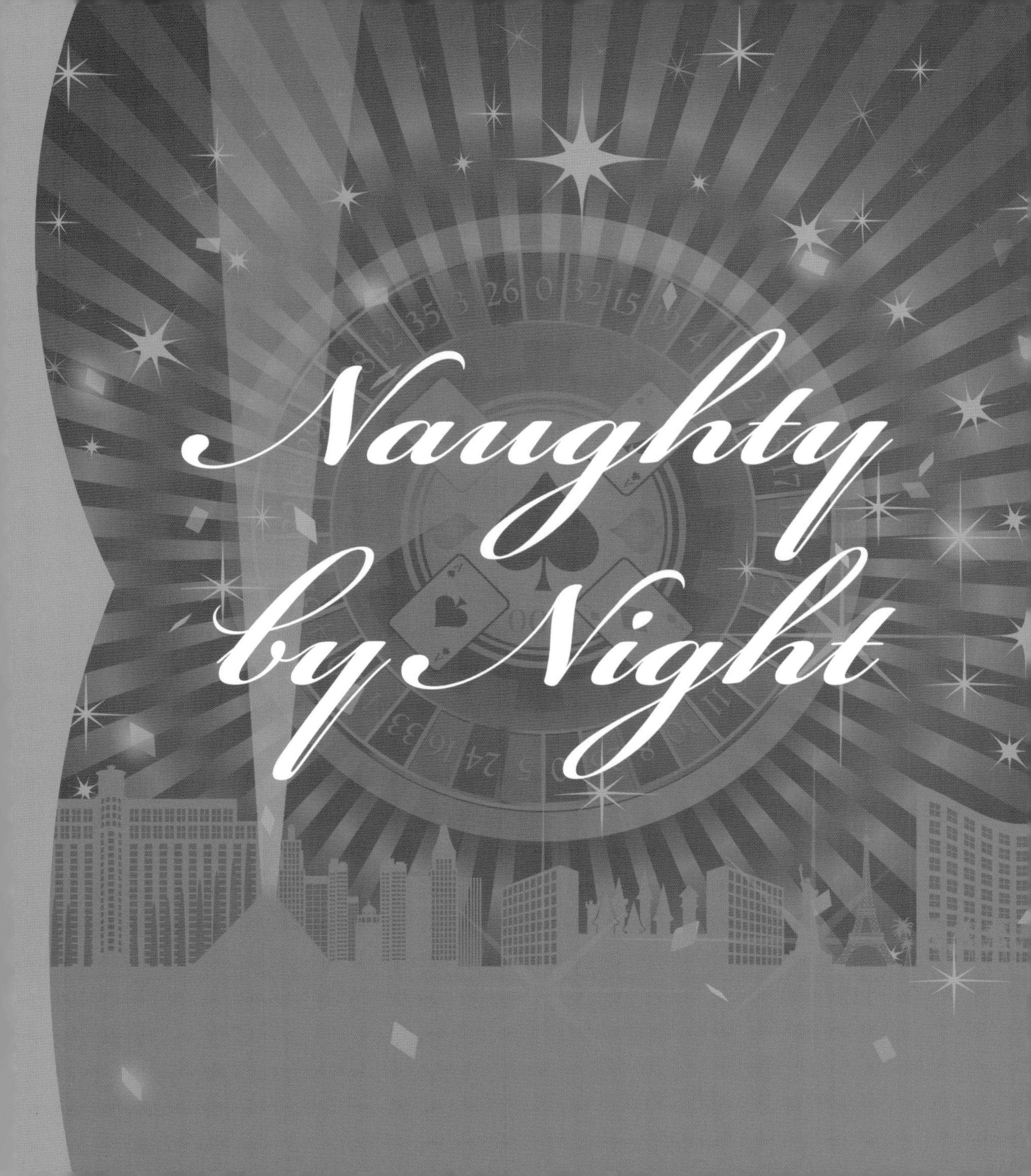
Naughty
by Night

PARIS HOTEL

NAUGHTY NIGHT TOURS

Check out these sexy night tours of Vegas on the next few pages—they aren't your typical sightseeing tours. Some involve tours of nightclubs in a party bus with a stripper pole and male strippers dancing for you; on other tours you can drink champagne in a limo while visiting male strip clubs. Sure you can tour Vegas on your own, but why not leave all the planning details in the hands of someone who really knows Vegas while you just relax and have the time of your life. Most of the companies will even customize your own naughty tour with your lover or girlfriends. You can even see if they can rearrange a package with ideas from my book by telling them the places you want to visit to see if they offer any deals.

SIN CITY PARTYS
888.903.9889
www.mysincityparty.com

Want to party like a rock star, a celebrity, or a naughty girl? Then check out Sin City Partys for your next night out on the town. They have some sexy packages, like the "Striptease Package," which gets you into a pole-dancing class and Olympic Gardens (a male and female strip club), and the "Chippendales Package," where you get free entry to the Chippendales show and much more. Or you can always make up your own. They'll help you work out the details and make sure your wild night goes off without a hitch.

TRENZ MIDNIGHT RUN
877.655.3330
www.trenzlasvegas.com

Trenz is a party planning service that lists many naughty packages, such as the "Midnight Run Male Stripper Booze Cruise," which is a bus full of champagne, stripper poles, great music, and hot guys dancing for you. You'll have to visit their website for a full list of packages, as there are too many to list. You can even customize your naughty package if they aren't naughty enough!

LAS VEGAS LIMO DIARIES
3867 S. Valley View Blvd., Suite 10A
702.530.7713
www.lasvegaslimodiaries.com

Las Vegas Limo Diaries are a series of articles, tips and other perspectives, offered by none other than the most professional and experienced of limo drivers. Who better to guide you through a night of sin-soaked fantasy than them! Also offered on the site are a variety of Limousine Packages, which include everything from stretch Hummers to Lincoln Town Cars. The sky is the limit with a completely naughty set of package tours, aptly titled: R, X, XX, XXX and finally, Custom. This site has plenty to offer for that perfect night in Sin City.

VEGAS PRIVATE SINS
1368 Valley View
702.243.7399
www.vegasprivatesins.com

Vegas Private Sins is geared to the VIP client who wants to taste Las Vegas in all of its hottest, most seductive and most unrestrained glory. They are the premiere choice, offering access to a nearly unlimited amount of VIP services, guaranteeing only the best dayclubs, nightclubs, limousine packages, gourmet dining and shows. This is the perfect avenue to choose for any type of bachelor/bachelorette party, or for those who want only the Ultimate Naughty Vegas Experience!

THE GREEN DOOR

SWINGING IN LAS VEGAS

If you're planning a naughty Las Vegas vacation, there are plenty of opportunities for you to fulfill your sexual fantasies. A lot of people are curious about swinging, and Las Vegas is probably one of the best cities in the country to dip your toes in the waters of the swinging lifestyle since it's legal here. There are many swinger clubs and gatherings in the city. Many are attended by first-timers who are looking to have some anonymous fun far from home. If you fall into that category, you can relax because a lot of people at the club are just as nervous as you may be. Most clubs don't serve alcohol, so you don't need to worry about being felt up by an obnoxious drunk. All the clubs have strict rules, and ignorance of these rules is not tolerated. You don't even have to play. If you're too nervous to snuggle with a stranger, you can watch and learn the ropes (so to speak). Some swinger clubs and parties have a photo screening process for membership, so be prepared to send in photos of you and your lover.

PURRFECT LAS VEGAS
www.purrfectlv.com

Purrfect Las Vegas is dedicated to creating upscale, safe and organized adult-themed events for those who want something a bit beyond the average club scenes and usual Vegas nightlife. These events have been a massive success and bring in droves of attractive and friendly crowds for socializing, dancing and sharing in adult-themed nights of adventure. They offer free and private memberships, so be sure to check their website often for upcoming events. Purrfect is perfect for the erotic socialite in all of us!

COUPLES OASIS
www.couplesoasis.com

Couples Oasis is an organization for swinging couples and those interested in the Lifestyle. If you are interested in this group, you must join their site, as The Couples Oasis Society is an online group that brings like-minded couples together. Once you have joined, you will have access to a variety of functions, events and parties that other members may be sponsoring or putting together. This group enjoys all sorts of activities and the emphasis is on getting people who are interested in swinging and the lifestyle together in a safe and respectful manner. If you are already a part of this group or simply curious, the Couples Oasis is surely a site to check out for all of your swinging needs!

KASIDIE
www.kasidie.com

This is an online community dedicated to swinging, BDSM, fetish lifestyle, and a lot more. You can find a lot of information on Las Vegas parties here. Plus you can build an anonymous online profile for free and find kinky couples, Masters, Mistresses, slaves, and more. They have extensive lists of swinger parties not only in Las Vegas, but also in other major cities worldwide. Their Swinger Club search engine is impressive. You can refine your search down to such details as the number of bathrooms in the club and if the D.J. is unpaid or professional.

VEGAS EXCHANGE
www.vegasexchange.com

If you're looking for a massive swinging event, they don't get much bigger than this. It's a huge swinging lifestyle convention and one of the biggest "lifestyle" events in the country. It's held over five days. They have kinky couples' workshops, and exhibitors selling all sorts of naughty toys, travel packages, and fetish items during the day. And at night they have sexy-themed parties at nightclubs and poolside. When you're ready for some action, just head upstairs to the many suites rented out for you and the other couples to get it on. And I don't mean just any suites, these are the best suites available. Some have their own pool, stripper poles, bowling alley, Barbie room, and more.

SWINGERS CIRCLE
www.swingerscircle.com

This group has parties every Thursday starting at 9:00 p.m. The location is announced two hours prior to the event. Like most swingers' clubs and parties, you have to join the group to find out where the "On the Strip Swingers Orgy Party" is located. Sex with other swingers is the norm. It's a limited event in terms of attendance—a maximum of 12 couples or women. Don't worry about creepy guys, because single guys aren't allowed.

PLUSH PARTIES
www.plushparties.net

Plush Parties bring you "Sexy Parties for Sexy People" and they host a variety of events geared to the swinging and adventurous set seeking elegant venues in which to mingle, socialize and "swing." Membership is private and signing up for their newsletter is recommended, as it is the only way to "be in the know" of the next upcoming parties. Plush Parties host huge events with around 2,000 guests and are held in sexy hotels and nightclubs. They are hosted all over California and they even host an annual event here in Sin City called "Dirty Vegas" where they take over Rumor Hotel with topless pool parties and naughty events at night.

RED ROOSTER
6405 Greyhound Ln.
702.451.6661
www.vegasredrooster.com

This is one of the oldest swingers' clubs in Las Vegas. It was established in the home of a swinger couple and has since grown to a big facility/party house. The hosts, Mike and Chris, request you be at least 25 years old to enter, but that's the only restriction on who can come to the party. They have parties every day, but check their website for times as they vary. They even have a band that plays Thursday to Saturday and they host weekly events. Make sure to read their rules before visiting as there are many things you need to know, such as bringing your own alcohol, making sure you don't arrive to the house early or during off hours, and much more.

THE GREEN DOOR
953 E. Sahara Ave.
702.732.4656/800.718.3794
www.greendoorlasvegas.com

They were founded in 1998 and are one of the most popular swingers' clubs in town. They have no application process and you don't need a sponsor. Just show up! They have a lovely "orgy room" and even a store where you can buy novelties and other fun, kinky things. They offer discounts through their website and for locals, and they host weekly events, so make sure to visit their website for details. If you're interested in renting out their entire club for a naughty party of your own, then give them a call.

FANTASY SWINGERS CLUB
953 E. Sahara Ave.
www.fantasyswingersclub.com

Fantasy Swingers Club is open seven days a week from 10 p.m. to 4 a.m. It's just off the Strip, so it's ideal if you're staying in a Strip hotel and are nervous about straying too far from your room for your naughty activity. They have a nice lounge area where you can chat up potential playmates before you get down and dirty. Once you do decide to jump in the naughty pool, so to speak, they have a lot of fun options like a full dungeon, a doctor's office, voyeur rooms, and even an orgy room.

LAS VEGAS AFTER DARK

You can get naughty in Las Vegas at any time of the day, but let's face it—nighttime is the best time to get your freak on. Something is always happening in the city, but Las Vegas at night is a world unto itself. The city has a different feel to it at night…a naughty one!

This chapter will take you on a tour of Las Vegas after dark. It is a world of strip clubs, drag queen shows, swinger parties, naughty escorts, burlesque shows, belly dancers, sexy diners, after-hour clubs for those who aren't ready to call it a night and more. So get ready for a naughty night to remember in Vegas!

SEXIEST RESTAURANTS

TAO AT THE VENETIAN

3355 S. Las Vegas Blvd.
702.388.8338
www.taolasvegas.com

This place is gorgeous! Once inside the restaurant, you'll notice a towering Buddha statue that seems to float in midair above a pool of water that's home to Japanese koi. They serve amazing pan-Asian food here and it's one of Las Vegas' hottest spots to see celebrities. It also has a super sexy bar where you can wait before being seated and hear live D.J. sets. One bit of advice: The bar at Tao gets packed (especially on weekends), but you can eat there if you can't get table reservations. The food is great for sharing with your lover or friends, and the restaurant is very lively. Plus if you have dinner at the restaurant, it gives you access to their nightclub. Another sexy spot you don't want to miss.

RED 8 AT WYNN
3131 S. Las Vegas Blvd.
702.770.3380
www.wynnlasvegas.com/restaurants/casualdining/red8

This sexy, red restaurant specializes in Asian cuisine. The color red and the number 8 are both considered lucky in Asian cultures, so you might just get lucky here! Walking into this restaurant will make you feel as if you've stepped into a geisha house. It has a nice, exotic, sexy feel to it. Their menu offers everything from traditional pad thai (my favorite dish here) to roast duck, and it's reasonably priced. Plus you don't need reservations, so you can walk right in.

STRIP HOUSE AT PLANET HOLLYWOOD

BLOSSOM AT ARIA
3730 S. Las Vegas Blvd.
877.230.2742
www.arialasvegas.com/dining/restaurants/blossom

They serve traditional Chinese cuisine here, and even offer a discounted early evening menu (and their tasting menu isn't too hard on your wallet either). The food is excellent and they have a bar right next door called the Baccarat Lounge where you can grab a quick drink before dinner. It's very sexy with lots of gold tones and lush furniture. My favorite spot there is a booth in one corner where you and your lover can snuggle up and do naughty things.

RED SQUARE AT MANDALAY BAY
3950 S. Las Vegas Blvd.
702.632.7407
www.mandalaybay.com/dining/red-square/

This is one of the best Russian restaurants in the city and allows you to take a peek behind the "Iron Curtain." It's decorated with deep reds and Soviet-era art. They only serve dinner here, so reservations are a good idea. They have an impressive selection of caviar, and you can get a free half-ounce when you buy two cocktails during their "cavi-hour." Be sure to check out their Frozen Ice Bar (made of ice!) and their Vodka Vault. It's amazing! The selection is top-notch, so don't miss out on this place.

STRIP HOUSE AT PLANET HOLLYWOOD

3667 S. Las Vegas Blvd.
702.737.5200
www.striphouse.com

It's not a strip club, instead it's one of the sexiest steak restaurants I've seen. Decorated with sexy vintage photos and pinups of 1920s flapper girls, you can't help but feel like you're in a sexy speakeasy. They have a nice wine list with a lot of organic vintages to choose from. Want something more decadent? How about a twenty-four-layer chocolate cake or potatoes made with goose fat instead of butter? The steaks are grade-A, too!

STRIP HOUSE AT PLANET HOLLYWOOD

JOEL ROBUCHON AT MGM GRAND
3799 S. Las Vegas Blvd.
702.891.7925
www.mgmgrand.com/restaurants/joel-robuchon-french-restaurant.aspx

Voted France's Chef of the Century, Joel Robuchon came out of retirement to open this Michelin three-star-rated restaurant. It is one of the most expensive restaurants in Vegas and Chef Robuchon's only fine dining restaurant in the United States. They treat you like royalty here, by picking you up and dropping you off in a limo (if it's available on the night you make reservations, so plan ahead). They take you through a private entrance and you get the chance to walk through The Mansion, which is a *very* private hotel attached to the MGM Grand (you can't make reservations for a room here, you have to be invited—which usually means you're a high roller). The restaurant is gorgeous! And the bread cart is to die for. Just be careful with how much bread you eat or else you'll be too full to enjoy your dinner and dessert.

HANK'S AT GREEN VALLEY RANCH
2300 Paseo Verde Pkwy., Henderson
702.617.7515
www.greenvalleyranch.sclv.com/dining/hanks.aspx

You can get some of the best steaks in town here, and it's away from a lot of the hustle and bustle of the Strip. Their martinis are excellent and their vintage décor is super sexy. You'll feel like you've stepped back into the 1960s. You could film an episode of *Mad Men* here and not have to change much. They have a nice happy hour from 4 p.m. to 6 p.m. and they've received many awards for their quality steaks.

T-BONES CHOPHOUSE AT THE RED ROCK CASINO RESORT & SPA
11011 W. Charleston Blvd.
702.797.7777
www.redrock.sclv.com/dining/t-bones-chophouse.aspx

This beautiful steakhouse was voted the best in Las Vegas in 2010 by *Las Vegas Review* readers. This sexy restaurant has high ceilings, gorgeous hardwood trimmings, a wine loft with over 7,000 bottles, fireplaces and candles throughout the place, and a gorgeous outdoor patio. Their meats are all-natural (just the way I like my meat!) and you can dine while overlooking the Red Rock's pool. Make sure to check out the Onyx Bar, as you can get a drink here while waiting for your table. It's a sexy bar with live D.J. music. Their "Martini Chill" nights offer live spins from local D.J.s and excellent martinis.

THE BARRYMORE AT THE ROYAL HOUSE
99 Convention Center Dr.
702.407.5303
www.barrymorelv.com

This sultry restaurant and bar is decked out in burgundies, bronzes, blacks, and chromes. It features tufted booths, mirrored walls, and damask wallpaper. The sensuous inside bar area looks like something they brought back from a 1920s speakeasy. They serve local craft beers, handcrafted cocktails, and a selection of fine wines from around the world, all under $50. Their outside patio is just as sexy, with a fireplace, lounge seating, and great views of Las Vegas.

HAKKASAN AT MGM
3799 S. Las Vegas Blvd.
702.891.3888
www.hakkasanlv.com

As the story goes, the staff at a popular Las Vegas club embarrassed the owner of Hakkasan by being rude, so he invested $200 million of his own money to create his own place where the staff is super friendly. Hakkasan, layered in its signature blue color, has a delightful Asian-themed menu, ambient music floating through the whole place, and these neat lattice screens (they call it "the Cage") that separate the dining area into several intimate areas. There's also a private dining area on the second level that overlooks the main floor. It's an all-in-one hot spot, as it has a restaurant, bar, and nightclub. The restaurant and bar are open everyday, and the nightclub is only open Thursday to Sunday.

ROSE.RABBIT.LIE. AT COSMOPOLITAN
3708 S. Las Vegas Blvd.
877.667.0585
www.roserabbitlie.com

A "communal venue that blurs the lines between restaurant, bar, club and live entertainment to create a grand social experiment." The venue is located on Level 2 of the West End Tower and is open from Wednesday to Saturday, from 5:30pm to the early morning hours. You can come when you want and leave when you want as there aren't any written rules here. This is a place you must experience for yourself as you never know what may happen.

CAPO'S
5675 W. Sahara Ave.
702.364.2276
www.caposrestaurant.com

This gorgeous Italian restaurant enforces a strict dress code and feels and looks like an old mob speakeasy. Reservations are highly recommended, even on a weekday night when you think it'll be slow. This place gets busy in the blink of an eye. It's mostly locals, but some tourists make it out here as it's located off the Strip. It's worth the drive and I highly recommend it. You will have to be buzzed in once you arrive and answer a few questions. Don't be surprised if it takes them awhile to answer the door. It's very old school here.

ANDREA'S AT ENCORE
3131 S. Las Vegas Blvd.
702.770.5340
www.wynnlasvegas.com/restaurants/finedining/andreas

This is a super fun place with lots of energy thanks to their D.J. spinning '80s and '90s music while people sing along and dance in their seats. They have an amazing drink list. I recommend the Lulu. The place is well-lit with lovely caramel colors and it has this big, sultry image of a woman's sexy eyes hanging behind the bar. The menu is Asian fusion, with stuff like a N.Y. Strip with a wasabi demi glace, duck confit lo mein, and a good sushi selection. They're also open late and have a great menu for after-hours dining.

MARRAKECH MOROCCAN RESTAURANT
3900 Paradise Rd.
702.737.5611
www.marrakechvegas.com

This restaurant has been in Vegas since 1979 and offers affordable dining (a six-course dinner for $40 each). This place is great to take your lover for an intimate dinner or a group of friends for a lively evening. Every night belly dancers perform while you enjoy dinner and drinks. You can even dance with the performers and take photos with them. And if you're looking for a venue to host your next naughty party of twenty people or more, then give them a call.

STRIP HOUSE AT PLANET HOLLYWOOD

SEXIEST BARS

LUCKY BAR AT RED ROCK
11011 W. Charleston Blvd., Summerlin
702.797.7777
www.redrock.sclv.com/entertainment/lounges-and-bars.aspx

If you want to be in the middle of the action, this is the bar for you. It's in the heart of the gaming floor at the Red Rock Casino. They serve great cocktails, and ladies drink free on Thursday nights! It has a neat layout, with a sleek feel and this neat lava lamp–like structure in the middle of the bar that extends up to the ceiling. They also have live D.J. sets Friday and Saturdays from 9 p.m. to 1 a.m., and there's no cover.

THE CHANDELIER BAR AT THE COSMOPOLITAN
3708 S. Las Vegas Blvd.
702.698.7000
www.cosmopolitanlasvegas.com/experience/lounges-and-bars/
chandelier.aspx

Part nightclub, part bar, part art sculpture—all amazing. The Cosmopolitan's Chandelier Bar is a must-see. It's a spectacular structure that's three stories high. Each level has a different bar "attached" to it. The chandelier drapes around each bar so it feels like you're having a drink inside this giant hanging glass art piece. The bottom level is a swinging, high-energy spot, the middle is a cocktail lounge, and the top is an ultra-modern and sexy bar that feels like something from the future.

VESPER BAR AT THE COSMOPOLITAN
3708 S. Las Vegas Blvd.
702.698.7000
www.cosmopolitanlasvegas.com/experience/lounges-and-bars/
vesper-bar.aspx

That's right, two sexy bars in the same casino hotel. Vesper Bar is named after the first love of James Bond and the martini she inspired. It's an exotic cocktail bar full of mirrored tiles and it has this amazing liquor cabinet that serves as the centerpiece of the bar. I don't know if spies hang out there, but you can certainly imagine it when you walk into the place. If you want an exotic cocktail lounge, go here.

LILY BAR & LOUNGE AT BELLAGIO
3600 S. Las Vegas Blvd.
702.693.8300
www.lilylv.com

If you're looking to get away from the hustle and bustle of the casino floors of Bellagio, then head over to Lily's. This bar and lounge is a beautiful place with panoramic views of the casino's gaming floors. It's a big place, almost 3,400 square feet, and it has these great big ottomans that are perfect for lounging with a lover. Dress sharp as you'll want to look your best at this bar because it's full of sexy people. It's also open until 4 a.m., so it's perfect for a nightcap before heading back to your hotel room with that special someone.

PORTOFINO AT THE MIRAGE
3400 S. Las Vegas Blvd.
702.792.7111
www.mirage.com/restaurants/portofino-by-chef-michael-laplaca.aspx

Chef Michael LaPlaca is the artist behind the authentic Italian cuisine found at Portofino, located in the iconic Mirage Hotel. Inspired by dishes from both land and sea, this restaurant boasts an extensive wine selection and an impressive menu. A warm and inviting decor permeates the restaurant, achieving a delicate blend of romance and elegance, making it a fantastic venue for a romantic dinner or drinks at the bar before hitting the Strip and embarking on the naughtier escapades of your evening.

GHOSTBAR AT PALMS
4321 W. Flamingo Rd.
702.942.7777
www.palms.com/nightlife/ghostbar

Found on the 55th floor of the Palms' Ivory Tower, Ghostbar has tall windows that give you great views of the city. There are luxurious tufted black leather couches perfect for lounging with friends or lovers. It has a sensual, sophisticated vibe with a white, black, and fuchsia color scheme. If you're adventurous, then head outside to the balcony. It has a glass floor so you're looking straight down at the Palms pool while you're over 500 feet above it. This place also turns into a dayclub during the winter months, with confetti showers and high-end beer pong, and they encourage you to wear costumes (www.palms.com/gbdc).

DROP BAR AT GREEN VALLEY RANCH
2300 Paseo Verde Pkwy., Henderson
702.617.7777
www.greenvalleyranch.sclv.com/Entertainment/Lounges-and-Bars.aspx

Drop Bar was voted "Best Lounge" in a 2011 *Las Vegas Journal-Review* poll. And it has to be one of the sexiest bars in Vegas with its deep purples, comfy sofas, and huge chandelier that hangs in the middle of the bar. Make sure to visit their website to check out all their specials. They offer happy hour everyday, Tequila Tuesdays, '80s-night specials on Thursday, Bloody Mary and mimosa specials on Saturday and Sunday mornings, and more.

EYE CANDY AT MANDALAY BAY
3950 S. Las Vegas Blvd.
877.632.7800
www.mandalaybay.com/entertainment/lounges/eyecandy-sound-lounge/

This sexy spot, located in the center of the casino, combines a sizzling nightclub with the newest modern technology for a hot experience. The club has a cool dance floor that constantly changes colors like in *Saturday Night Fever*. And the tables have interactive touch controls that allow you to create and project visuals and messaging onto screens above the dance floor. Spot a hottie on the dance floor? Then send them a message they can see. And best of all, there's no cover or lines to get in.

LAVO AT PALAZZO
3325 S. Las Vegas Blvd.
702.791.1800
www.lavolv.com

This is one of the hottest spots in Las Vegas, with gorgeous views of the strip from Lavo's terrace. They're open six nights a week, late into the evening. I'm talking hardcore partying late. They have a nightclub above the restaurant and lounge, so you can have drinks and a gourmet meal then burn it off at their sexy club. What makes this place sexy is their bar and lounge area. With hanging lamps that feel as if they're floating, muted colors, intimate seating, and low lighting, you'll feel as if you've stepped into an exotic location.

BACCARAT LOUNGE AT ARIA

3730 S. Las Vegas Blvd.
702.590.7757
www.arialasvegas.com/nightlife/bars-lounges/baccarat-lounge

This hidden gem in Aria is incredibly sexy and located right next to Blossom, which is one of the sexiest restaurants in town. It's a perfect place to have an intimate drink before dinner. It's decorated in gold and other warm colors, so you'll want to sink into a lounge chair and let your inner naughty girl get her groove on. There's a nook in the corner with a private booth to get frisky with your lover.

FIZZ LAS VEGAS AT CAESARS PALACE

3570 S. Las Vegas Blvd.
702.776.3200
www.fizzlv.com

In the heart of the iconic and legendary Caesars Palace, you will find FIZZ Las Vegas, a champagne lounge and bar and the epicenter of all that is chic. FIZZ is the celebration of the crossroads found between art, culture and fashion, and champagne and couture cocktails. Featuring a wide selection of artfully curated, high-end champagnes by the glass and set in a spectacular ambience teeming with '70s style, reflected in the rich golds and muted tones, Fizz is the perfect place for a pre- or post-show cocktail and socializing. Exquisite offerings of caviar, charcuterie and small plates make the perfect complement for the seductive libations offered here.

THE LADY SILVIA
900 S. Las Vegas Blvd., Downtown
702.405.0816
www.theladysilvia.com

This relaxed, sexy speakeasy has delicious cocktails and happy-hour specials everyday from 5 p.m. to 7 p.m. If you want a bar with a local crowd and background music, then check out this place. Their site describes it like this: "Inspired by Prague's Strahov Monastery Library, this lounge flaunts dazzling furniture situated on its black-and-white checkerboard floor, invoking an English-style library and cocktail bar ambiance." Located downtown, this venue has no visible signage and is tucked away in the SoHo Lofts, making you feel as if you've come across a hidden treasure.

MINUS5 ICE BAR
Two locations: 3930 S. Las Vegas Blvd./702.740.5800
3771 S. Las Vegas Blvd./702.643.7800
www.minus5experience.com

Located at both Mandalay Bay and Monte Carlo, Minus5 is a fabulous destination for a date or pre-dinner drinks. Come chill out at this sexy, cool bar where cuddling with your lover is mandatory! Inside this winter wonderland of hip ice sculpture and interactive ice architecture, even the cocktail glasses are made of ice. Actually, everything about this unique experience is crafted from ice: the walls, the bar and even the seats. With an ice sculptor working year round, creating new visualizations and themes, Minus5 is a must see. Gloves and coats are provided.

CHATEAU NIGHTCLUB AT PARIS HOTEL

SEXIEST CLUBS

XS AT ENCORE
3131 S. Las Vegas Blvd.
702.770.0097
www.xslasvegas.com

XS has a huge, gorgeous patio attached to it, and the nightclub has a nice wide-open feel to match. The club has five bars and special roped-off VIP areas with first-class service. The patio has over twenty poolside cabanas, blackjack tables, and, of course, the pool. If you're looking for primarily all house and electronic music, then this is your place. They are open Friday to Monday, and suggest if you reserve table service to show up early for better table availability.

TRYST AT WYNN
3131 S. Las Vegas Blvd.
702.770.3375
www.trystlasvegas.com

You know you're in for a sexy time when the name of the club means "secret meeting." It's layered in rich reds and situated along a private lagoon under a ninety-foot, three-tier waterfall. Looking for a threesome? Then make sure to order their drink Ménage a Trois, which features Grand Marnier and 24K gold flakes. Looking for a big dance floor with a famous D.J.? Then check out their event schedule online as lot of famous D.J.s play here, such as Afrojack, Skrillex, Deadmau5, and Steve Aoki.

GOLD BOUTIQUE NIGHTCLUB & LOUNGE AT ARIA
3730 S. Las Vegas Blvd.
702.693.8300
www.aria.com/nightlife/gold-boutique-nightclub-and-lounge

This gorgeous, intimate venue looks a bit like a Hollywood speakeasy inside, with lots of mirrored walls and royal red carpet. It was designed by Cirque du Soleil's design team (which took inspiration from Graceland). If you're an '80s fan, like myself, then this is your spot as they play all '80s music on Friday nights! Other nights they host D.J.s and special events, so check out their calendar online.

TAO AT THE VENETIAN
3355 S. Las Vegas Blvd.
702.388.8338
www.taolasvegas.com

Besides being one of the sexiest restaurants, Tao is also one of the sexiest nightclubs. It has a huge terrace that gives you a great view of the Strip and fantastic sound systems in two big rooms that play all sorts of dance music. They also have sexy go-go dancers, aerialists, and half-naked girls in a bathtub. And if you're looking to host a bachelorette party, then this is your place. They have special packages such as the "Bachelorette Final Fling," "Bachelorette Blowout," "Brides Night Out VIP Table Service," and "Ultimate VIP Stagette."

BEACHER'S MADHOUSE AT MGM

3799 S. Las Vegas Blvd.
877.880.0880
www.beachersmadhouse.com

Beacher's Madhouse is a tour de force of zany, wild theatrical action that has elevated itself to new heights at its MGM location. Originating a decade ago with Jeff Beacher's comedy shows in NYC, which were an instant success, it only made sense to take this kind of show to Las Vegas and with the MGM Grand hosting, Beacher's Madhouse takes on a whole new sense of style and flair. Featuring an ever-revolving cast of characters, many of whom are midgets and circus performers, Beacher's shows are laced with sex appeal, shock and comedy, creating a pioneering, new club experience that is an absolute must see. You won't be able to contain yourself!

FOUNDATION ROOM AT MANDALAY BAY

3950 S. Las Vegas Blvd.
702.632.7631
www.houseofblues.com/lasvegas/fr

This gorgeous steakhouse/nightclub is layered in Asian themes, antique chandeliers, and exotic artwork wherever you look. It's associated with the House of Blues, so don't be surprised if you see a famous musician or two there. They also have a beautiful bar where you can have drinks before or after dinner. The bar turns into a hopping nightclub playing '80s, '90s, top 40s and R&B music, and has a stellar view of the Strip. Be sure to check out the Ganesh Room.

CHATEAU AT PARIS
3655 S. Las Vegas Blvd.
702.776.7770
www.chateaunights.com

This is one of my favorite nightclubs. They offer incredible views of the Bellagio fountain from their gorgeous Chateau Rooftop Garden. And the most amazing view is of The Eiffel Tower, which sits on top of the Rooftop Garden. I think this is the best spot in the entire club. It's outside so you have great views, cool breeze (if it's not summertime), and fresh air. Plus their VIP areas are very sexy with white tufted booths, chandeliers, and mirrors. Their inside club is just as sexy with deep purples, black tufted VIP booths, a fireplace, and huge hanging chandeliers over the dance floor.

PURE AT CAESARS
3570 S. Las Vegas Blvd.
702.731.7873
http://hakkasangroup.com/nightlife-daylife/pure/

Offering great views of the Strip, this 40,000-square-foot club is actually four clubs in one. Each of the four rooms (with all-white décor tinged with reds, pinks, and purples) has a different D.J. or theme for the night. It's great for dancing, either in one of the D.J. rooms or under the sky on the patio. Smoking is allowed here, but you can always have fun on the patio if it gets too thick inside one of the D.J. rooms. Ladies often get in free, and your boyfriend can sometimes get a free pass if you're near the club a couple hours before they open the doors.

THE BANK AT BELLAGIO
3600 S. Las Vegas Blvd.
702.693.8300
www.thebanklasvegas.com

This club plays great Top 40 and R&B music and has the best air conditioner system in any nightclub in Las Vegas. I once danced here all night and never sweated! It's a small and intimate place with tons of people dancing; which means it should get hot in there, but I never was hot the entire night. It's best to get VIP service because of the club's small size. It gets packed in there (which means there are plenty of hot bodies to rub against!), and the dance floor is small as well. The only places to stand, if you don't have a VIP table, are the dance floor and bar area.

PURE NIGHTCLUB AT CAESARS

BODY ENGLISH AT HARD ROCK HOTEL
4455 Paradise Rd.
702.693.5555
www.bodyenglish.com

This exotic club oozes sex appeal with its red couches, dark hardwoods, and a big dance floor. Their VIP booths are cozy and offer nice views of the dance floors. They have a Parlor room, if you want something more private. Their D.J.s are top-notch, and a lot of hip-hop artists and musicians host parties here.

DRAG SHOWS

FRANK MARINO'S DIVAS LAS VEGAS AT THE QUAD
3535 S. Las Vegas Blvd.
855.234.7469/702.794.3311
www.thequadlv.com/shows/Frank-marinos-divas-las-vegas.html

Located at the Quad hotel, Mr. Marino is perhaps Las Vegas' best-known female impersonator, and his show is a dazzling array of drag performers. The show is high-energy, reasonably priced, and a lot of fun. You'll swear some of the performers are the celebrities they're imitating. You'll see "Janet Jackson, "Madonna," "Tina Turner," "Liza Minelli," and many others. Frank Marino himself starts the show as "Joan Rivers" and makes so many costume changes during the show that your head will spin. I don't know how he puts on those elaborate gowns and wigs so fast!

CHARLIE'S LAS VEGAS
5012 Arville St.
702.876.1844
www.charlieslasvegas.com

This Western-themed gay bar caters to bears, cowboys who like other cowboys, and hunks without shirts. It also has some fun drag events like free Drag Queen Bingo on Tuesdays (with lots of opportunities for free shots!) and Charlie's Amazing Drag Review on Sundays—which is a four-hour drag show that has good drink specials to go with it.

FLAMBOYANCE
4371 W. Charleston Blvd.
702.385.3539
www.flamboyanceshow.com / www.flexlasvegas.com

Located just four miles from the Strip, Flex Cocktail Lounge is known for friendly bartenders, and good prices on their cocktails. They're also known for drag queen karaoke and the FlamBOYance performers. FlamBOYance is a weekly drag show on Thursday nights that has no cover and a different theme every week. Their shows range from classic drag shows to celebrity look-alike shows and "fucked-up fairy tales." You can also hire their cast members to perform at your events.

SEXY COMEDY SHOWS

SIN CITY COMEDY SHOW AT PLANET HOLLYWOOD
3667 S. Las Vegas Blvd.
702.777.2782
www.sincitycomedy.com

This show is sexy because it mixes comedy with sexy burlesque performers. You'll be in stitches for one set, and squirming in your seat (in a good way) the next. Come for a good laugh, sexy dancers, and a stiff drink. The show is on the mezzanine level of Planet Hollywood with daily performances at 7 p.m. and 9 p.m., so come before or after dinner.

MENOPAUSE: THE MUSICAL AT THE LUXOR
3900 S. Las Vegas Blvd.
702.262.4400/800.557.7428
www.luxor.com/entertainment/entertainment_menopause.aspx

Four women at a lingerie party crack jokes and sing songs about "the change," their sex lives, and much more. It's one of the longest-running shows and for a good reason: it's really funny. It's a ninety-minute show that includes twenty-five re-lyricized songs from the '60s and '70s. Showtimes are Wednesday to Monday at 5:30 p.m., and Tuesday at 8 p.m.

BELLY DANCING SHOWS

MARRAKECH
3900 Paradise Rd., Suite Y
702.737.5611
www.marrakechvegas.com

This Moroccan restaurant has nightly belly dancing shows that encourage audience participation. Some of their dancers have performed across the world. They sometimes incorporate comedy into the show if someone seems nervous. Plus the food is excellent here. It's served Moroccan style with low tables surrounded by pillows and the staff makes you feel very welcome.

ALI BABA LAS VEGAS
8826 S. Eastern Ave.
702.688.4182
www.alibabalasvegas.com

This Lebanese restaurant features not only good food and gorgeous dancers, but also live musicians and singers. It has a Middle Eastern–style nightclub inside, and it is the only such club in the city. The performers there are famous in their home countries and put on an amazing show. They dance until dawn some nights, so be ready for a workout!

THE MASSIVE SPECTACULAR
www.themassivespectacular.com

This annual charity event, in March, benefits the Nevada Childhood Cancer Foundation. It's an amazing night full of beautiful belly dancers from around the world. Make sure to book in advance for this event and make a weekend out of it by booking a belly dancing class and one of the belly-dancing dinners in this book.

PORN-STAR KARAOKE

KARAOKE XXX
332 W. Sahara Ave.
702.382.6288/702.900.6888
www.karaokexxx.com

If you're looking for something different to do in Vegas, then this is definitely it. Every Monday night at The Red Label, you can karaoke alongside some of your favorite porn stars. Or treat your lover to a night of naughtiness where the both of you can check out the sexy talent. Visit their website to view a weekly list of who will be hosting for the evening. Everyone is welcome and if you're interested in learning more about the adult industry or how to get started, then this is a great place to network.

NAUGHTY KARAOKE
www.facebook.com/karaokevegas

Party with Porn Stars on those hot, triple X nights! Naughty Karaoke is dedicated to bringing people together with a passion for hot, sexy girls and karaoke! Naughty Karaoke hosts multiple events in Las Vegas each week, which you can access through their site. They host at all the hottest and trendiest Las Vegas Nightclubs, and also offer Stripper Karaoke and Bikini'Oke. So, if you want to get out, party and sing that favorite song of yours with the hottest women in Vegas, then this is most definitely a site to check out. These events are fun, super naughty and perfect for large groups!

NAUGHTY CIRCUS-STYLE SHOWS

ZUMANITY AT NYNY
3790 S. Las Vegas Blvd.
702.740.6815
www.cirquedusoleil.com/en/shows/zumanity/default.aspx

This is a Cirque du Soleil show, so you know the performers and visuals will be world-class. This show promotes itself as "the sensual side of Cirque du Soleil," so that takes the beauty up a notch or two. It not only has the acrobatics and dance that make Cirque du Soleil famous, but it adds burlesque to the mix! They make no secret that this show is adult-themed, so don't come in expecting to see something approved by your local Sunday-school

teachers (although you may see many of them in the audience!). They're dark on Wednesdays and Thursdays, so make sure to book early.

ABSINTHE AT CAESARS PALACE
3570 S. Las Vegas Blvd.
800.745.3000
www.absinthevegas.com

Part-burlesque show, part-cabaret, part-magic show, part-cult movie, *Absinthe* is one of Las Vegas' newest shows and one of the hottest tickets in town. If you like your burlesque a little bizarre, don't miss it. Acrobats, roller skaters, and a lot of lovely, sultry women perform in the round for your pleasure. The women are all exotic beauties not afraid to show off their curves. Lounge singers sing for you, beautiful women tantalize you, and strong men wow you. It has something for everyone in a circus-style tent.

X-BURLESQUE AT FLAMINGO

STRIPTEASE SHOWS

X-BURLESQUE AT FLAMINGO
3555 S. Las Vegas Blvd.
702.777.2782
www.flamingolasvegas.com/shows/x-burlesque.html

This show is full of exotic, sexy women (many of whom can be seen dancing around the blackjack tables, or even dealing blackjack, at the Flamingo) performing nightly to hot music. They have a fun bathtub routine and they are all sexy and attractive. Working at X-Burlesque was voted among the "12 Sexiest Jobs" by the E! Channel, so that's a great endorsement. Stay after the show so you can get your photo taken with some of the dancers.

FANTASY AT LUXOR
3900 S. Las Vegas Blvd.
702.262.4400
www.fantasyluxor.com

This show has been running for 12 years and also was voted "Best Showgirls" in a 2012 Las Vegas poll. They perform seven days a week and claim to be "the Strip's biggest tease." Naughty cops, naughty schoolgirls, naughty conga players, and naughty pole dancers all shimmy and shake for your pleasure. Also, if you want to enjoy a sexy dinner before the show, Rice & Company at the Luxor offers a three-course meal of Flirty Beginnings, Seductive Temptations, and Exotic Encore all for a great price including tickets to Fantasy.

PIN UP AT THE STRATOSPHERE
2000 S. Las Vegas Blvd.
702.380.7777
www.stratospherehotel.com/Hotel/Nightlife/Shows/PIN-UP

This show is hosted by *Playboy Magazine*'s 2011 Playmate of the Year, Claire Sinclair. So, head up the Strip to the Stratosphere to see Miss Sinclair and her six-piece band in a fun, naughty show. If you're a fan of timeless glamour of the '40s, '50s, and '60s pinup, then you'll love this cheeky, sexy show.

MALE REVUES

CHIPPENDALES AT RIO
3700 W. Flamingo Rd.
702.777.7776
www.chippendales.com

This theatre was designed by women for women, and it's full of hot male dancers. The *Las Vegas Review Journal* named it the best male strip show in the city, and its reputation is well earned. It's a big theatre and great for girls-only and bachelorette parties. When you purchase a ticket they come with free admission to Rio's Voodoo Lounge and Caesars Pure Nightclub. The Chippendales' club also has a great bar of their own, Flirt Lounge, where you can drink before and after the show and meet some of the performers. Make sure to visit their website for special guests.

THUNDER FROM DOWN UNDER AT EXCALIBUR
3850 S. Las Vegas Blvd.
702.597.7600
www.thunderfromdownunder.com

I don't know what's in the water in Australia, but they breed some of the hottest guys in the world there. This all-male revue show comes from the land down under and was voted "Best Male Revue" in 2011. So be prepared to be "Thunderstruck" as these men strip down to barely there costumes. They perform a ninety-minute show every night, eleven shows weekly, and they offer special party packages including custom ones if they aren't naughty enough for you. And make sure to visit their website for some of the sexiest photos of naked men in their "Thunder Fans" section.

THUNDER FROM DOWN UNDER AT EXCALIBUR

MEN THE EXPERIENCE AT RIVERIA
2901 S. Las Vegas Blvd.
702.794.9525
www.mentheexperience.com

These athletic men will stun you with a wonderfully classy and upscale show that is torn straight from the pages of your most treasured Romance Novel. Sit back and be charmed by the parade of cowboys, secret agents, gangsters and so much more that come to life before your eyes. The audience also gets to participate in this show, so be ready when that sexy hunk comes looking for you! This is a great, old-school Vegas show that hits the spot for couples or a group of your favorite gals, no matter what the occasion.

TOPLESS SHOWS

JUBILEE! AT BALLY'S
3645 S. Las Vegas Blvd.
855.234.7469/702.777.2782
www.ballyslasvegas.com/shows/Jubilee.html

Winner of "Best Showgirls" in a 2012 Las Vegas poll, Jubilee is one of the longest-running (nearly thirty years!) and best-known burlesque shows in town. It's also the last authentic showgirl show. If you want to see beautiful women in sparkly, feathered costumes that cost thousands of dollars, this is the show for you. They have over one-hundred performers, many of whom perform topless. This is classic Vegas at its naughtiest. Shows are held every night except Fridays. Showtimes are Sunday to Wednesday at 7 p.m. and 10 p.m., Thursday at 7 p.m., and Saturday at 10 p.m.

CRAZY GIRLS AT RIVIERA
2901 S. Las Vegas Blvd.
702.794.9433
www.rivierahotel.com/las-vegas-entertainment/crazy-girls.aspx

This famous topless revue has been entertaining men and women for over twenty-five years. They keep the show lighthearted and classy. It's a nice cabaret atmosphere with some "old-school Vegas" charm. They have a comedian between the girls' acts, some magic, and some fun solo performances that include acrobatics.

X ROCKS AT RIO
3700 W. Flamingo Rd.
702.777.7776
www.riolasvegas.com/shows/x-rock.html

This show combines topless, erotic dancers with high-energy rock 'n' roll. If you like metal, classic rock, and alternative grunge rock, you will like this show. Exotic women dance to songs by Alice in Chains, Alice Cooper, Black Sabbath, and the like. A comedian entertains the crowd between acts. One sexy routine features three exotic women on chairs that look like choppers. The show is open Thursday to Sunday and starts at 10 p.m.

BURLESQUE SHOWS

LIVE BURLESQUE IN LAS VEGAS
3200 West Sirius Ave.
702.368.1863
www.liveburlesqueinlasvegas.com

Usually happening the last Saturday of every month, the simply titled "Live Burlesque in Las Vegas" troupe brings neo and classical burlesque performances to packed crowds at Boomer's Bar. Make sure to get there early to reserve a seat, or call ahead to reserve a VIP booth. They do a lot of fun-themed shows, like a Halloween and an '80s-flashback show.

LOU LOU ROXY
www.facebook.com/pages/Lou-Lou-Roxy-Burlesque/114420318631339

Lou Lou Roxy, founding member of the Las Vegas Grind Kittens, is a burlesque entertainer, singer, dancer, makeup artists and performer who has been working in Vegas for the last ten years. She has been featured in a variety of vaudeville and burlesque shows around town, bringing a captivating mixture of crowd-pleasing striptease, fetish performance and character art to life on the stage. Recently, Lou Lou was added to the roster at Las Vegas Burlesque Classes studio and is also available for private lessons. Be sure to check out one of Lou Lou's one-of-a-kind stage shows by visiting her website and Facebook page to view her calendar.

ZOMBIE BURLESQUE
3363 Las Vegas Blvd.
866.932.1818
www.zombieburlesqueshow.com

Come and experience the Zombie Burlesque event of a lifetime in this hilarious 'undead' musical on the Strip. A truly unique and innovative show, the plot unfolds as the Undead and the Living have struck an arrangement to exist in harmony together, circa 1958 in Las Vegas, and as an act of good faith, the Zombies have opened the door to their premiere nightclub, Club Z, to humans! Watch as a dazzling cast of the most talented performers and dancers entertain you with a high-energy show of humor, dance and nonstop sex appeal! It is one of the most popular shows playing on the Strip currently, so be sure to make reservations. Highly recommended!

BURLESQUE LAS VEGAS
www.burlesquelv.com

Visit here for all things burlesque in Las Vegas. This isn't a club or a show. It's a website that works as a big information center for Las Vegas burlesque culture. You can view their calendar to find out where burlesque shows are being performed around the city. They also list weekly burlesque classes if you want to learn the craft.

NAUGHTY CASINOS

Looking for somewhere naughty in Vegas to play blackjack or poker? You may not be able to find casino's where they have scantily clad dealers. Unfortunately, Sin City won't allow topless women to deal cards just yet, but a few casinos have lovely ladies in lingerie dealing out a river or spinning a roulette wheel. You already know the odds are stacked against you at the tables, so why not lose your money to a sexy lady who's easy on the eyes and will make you feel a little better about not being able to afford cab fare back to your hotel that night.

THE PLEASURE PIT AT PLANET HOLLYWOOD
3667 S. Las Vegas Blvd.
877.333.9474
www.planethollywoodresort.com

The Pleasure Pit is decorated in lovely pink lights and even lovelier ladies. They have pole dancers between the rows of gambling tables to entertain you, and the dealers all wear black, red, and pink lingerie. Most of the dealers wear corsets and hot pants, but the pole dancers wear even less.

The best time to be at the Pleasure Pit is at 8:00 p.m. This is when the dealers and dancers change shifts. If you can get to the escalators that connect to the mezzanine level, you can watch over thirty lovely ladies come down the escalator and then parade to the Pit. It's one of the best free naughty shows in town!

PUSSYCAT DOLLS CASINO AT CAESARS PALACE
3570 S. Las Vegas Blvd.
702.731.7110
www.caesarspalace.com

Added to the classic casino in 2009, the Pussycat Dolls Casino combines the sensuous Pussycat Dolls burlesque show with table gambling and slots. It's located in the PURE club and right across from the PCD lounge, so it's easy to find. They have pole and cage dancers performing in the middle of the pit, and the dealers all look like they just stepped offstage from

THE PLEASURE PIT AT PLANET HOLLYWOOD

a sexy show. One fun feature is that some of the table legs look like real ladies' legs complete with fishnet stockings and high heels.

They also have a nice shift-change tradition in which the girls parade around the entire pit clapping their hands and getting everyone fired up and happy. They wear different colored lingerie from the previous shift, so it's an eye-popping display.

RIO ALL-SUITES HOTEL AND CASINO

VEGAS AFTER-HOURS

We've all heard that expression about Sin City: It's a city that never sleeps. It's true! There are tons of things to do even when the clubs close. So if you want to make it out this late, make sure to sleep all day. Wake up around 5 p.m., get ready, head to dinner or a show, then to a nightclub for dancing, and then to an after-hours club, strip club, or late-night dinner. If you're a night owl and would rather hang out with the real partygoers at 3 a.m. instead of the tourists at 3 p.m., then read on for some fun things you can do while everyone else is stumbling back to their hotel room at 2 a.m., because you'll be stumbling back at 7 a.m.

DANCING & DRINKS

DRAI'S AT CROMWELL
3595 S. Las Vegas Blvd.
702.737.0555
www.drais.net

The new Cromwell hotel now hosts one of the hottest nightclubs in Las Vegas, Drai's. It's an all-in-one club serving as a Beach Club and Nightclub with 65,000-square-feet of indoor and outdoor space with stunning views of the Strip. For those of you not ready to call it a night, make sure to visit the famous *Drai's After Hours* club located in the basement of the Cromwell hotel. Doors may open at 1 a.m. for the after-hours club, however the party doesn't get started until 3 or 4 a.m.

PEPPERMILL FIRESIDE LOUNGE
2985 Las Vegas Blvd.
702.735.4177
www.peppermilllasvegas.com

Open 24 hours a day, the Fireside Lounge has a neat vibe to it with cool décor, great cocktails, and a big round fireplace. They serve food all day long (including breakfast), so it's a great place to get an omelet, steak, burger, or cup of coffee to recharge after a long night out.

ARTISAN
1501 W. Sahara Ave.
800.554.4092
www.artisanhotel.com

This place was voted sexiest boutique hotel and best place to go topless by the pool in a recent city survey, so you can expect their after-hours club to be just as sexy. Hot D.J.s and jumping crowds are here nightly, so it's a good place to get your late-night freak on. They are open 24/7. On weekdays you can hang out at the bar, lounge, or heated outdoor patio. On weekends check out their infamous, award-winning ultra-parties.

FOOD & DRINKS

SUGAR FACTORY AT PARIS HOTEL
3655 S. Las Vegas Blvd.
702.331.5100
www.sugarfactorylv.com

Located in the Paris Hotel on the Strip, this wonderful eatery is always open (24/7) and serves a wide variety of items, including gourmet steaks, customized cakes, and delicious milkshakes. It won the 2012 OpenTable diner's choice award, so it comes highly recommended. Also, I've eaten at this place many late nights and can personally vouch for it!

MR. LUCKY'S AT HARD ROCK
4455 Paradise Rd.
702.693.5592
www.hardrockhotel.com/las-vegas-restaurants/24-7-diner

If you're stumbling back from one of Hard Rock's nightclubs or the casino, you may need a pick-me-up meal and drink. Mr. Lucky's is open all hours and is a retro-style diner. They have a full-service menu that includes spiked milkshakes, burgers, and breakfast around the clock. And you're not too far away from all the action. They have great views of the casino floor, perfect for people watching while you're chowing down.

GRAND LUX CAFÉ AT VENETIAN
Two Locations: 3327 S. Las Vegas Blvd./702.733.7411
3355 S. Las Vegas Blvd./702.414.3888
www.grandluxcafe.com

There are two of these great cafés in Vegas, one at the Palazzo and one at the Venetian. At the Venetian the Grand Lux Café is open 24 hours a day. They serve a delicious menu, including items such as the "Red Velvet Pancakes" made with a hint of cocoa, chocolate chips, and cream-cheese frosting. Yum! They also have a nice wine list if you're up for a late-night bottle. If you don't feel like eating at the restaurant, get your order "to go" by calling ahead or ordering at the bakery counter.

CENTRAL AT CAESARS PALACE
3570 S. Las Vegas Blvd.
702.650.5921
www.centrallv.com

Central (pronounced sen-TRAL) is a beautiful late-night eatery with a double-sided full bar, where you can order specialty cocktails. It also has an outdoor patio terrace. Located in Caesars Palace, this all-night casual place is run by renowned chef Michel Richard and features amazing French-Californian fusion cuisine. Where else are you going to get a lobster burger at 2 a.m.?

THE HENRY AT THE COSMOPOLITAN
3708 S. Las Vegas Blvd.
702.698.7000
www.cosmopolitanlasvegas.com

Located inside the palatial Cosmopolitan Hotel on the Strip, The Henry is a sexy late-night eatery for those who are hungry after clubbing all night. Open 24/7 and presenting a dazzling collection of classic, reinterpreted variations of old-school, strip-style standards, The Henry is the perfect place to end a night of drunken revelry. Fresh ingredients, classic style and amiable service are all at your beck and call in this New Vegas mainstay.

STRIP CLUBS

It's no surprise that a town that flaunts sex would be a haven for strip clubs. Las Vegas has enough of them to host scores of bachelor parties at the same time every night of the week. Some of the best strip clubs in the country are here. Many feature top-level performers, adult movie stars, and even your favorite Internet model now and then.

Strip clubs in Las Vegas aren't just for men. Women can have just as much fun as the guys in a strip club. Whether it's a bachelorette party, a girl-friends' getaway, a birthday bash, or no reason at all (other than you wanting to see naked men . . . or women), you can check out the many places featuring sexy dancers. Women are much sexier to look at than men, in my opinion; but if you want male eye candy, there are strip clubs just for you (and gay men, for that matter).

SPEARMINT RHINO
3340 S. Highland Dr.
702.796.3555
www.spearmintrhinolv.com

This is one of my personal favorites. Full disclosure: I used to work there! It has the best-quality dancers and there's plenty of eye candy. They have over one-hundred girls working throughout the night. They also offer free limousine service and some amazing package deals for the back rooms.

HUSTLER CLUB
6007 Dean Martin Dr.
702.795.3131
www.vegashustlerclub.com

Want a Sexy Party? A Porn Party? A *Bed Party*? They have them all at Larry Flynt's Hustler Club. They can reserve special seating areas for group parties, and even make you a guest of honor on stage. The Hustler Club also hosts some wild events, such as "Topless Glow Party" and "Sindustry Sunday" with open bar and buffet. If you want to be featured in Hustler magazine, then head out to their "Hustler Honey" search on Monday nights. And if you're a local, then you always get in free!

SAPPHIRE
3025 Industrial Rd.
702.796.6000
www.sapphirelasvegas.com

They claim to be the largest strip club in the world and they may be right. The place has 70,000 square feet and has ten skyboxes upstairs where you can overlook the venue. They have male dancers Fridays and Saturdays from 9:30 p.m. until 1:00 a.m. For $90.00 per girl, you can throw a wild bachelorette party here that will get you a limo ride, VIP seating, a dance for the bride-to-be on stage, and a lot more.

HUNK MANSION
6007 Dean Martin Dr.
702.932.8625
www.hunkmansion.com

Located in Larry Flynt's Hustler Club, Hunk Mansion is a small, intimate nightclub with an elegant decor. Gorgeous and fantastically ripped professional and amateur dancers give performances throughout the night in this dimly lit monument to masculinity. You can also buy a ticket to ride on an exhilarating, six-foot mechanical penis, or you can simply have your picture taken on it for a great naughty Vegas souvenir. Perfect for bachelorette parties or a fun-filled girls' night out!

TREASURES
2801 Westwood Dr.
702.257.3030
www.treasureslasvegas.com

This club claims to be "the most luxurious gentlemen's club in the world." It's a bold claim, and the décor of the place certainly backs it up. The private lounges are like miniature clubs within the club. The Champagne Room even has private restrooms. They also have a steakhouse here that looks like one you'd find at a high-end casino hotel. They serve lobster, filet mignon, chicken Marsala, and other fantastic dishes while you check out the other, ahem, dishes on display.

THE PALOMINO CLUB
1848 N. Las Vegas Blvd.
877.399.2023
www.palominolv.com

The Palomino Club is a big place (30,00 square feet). It's been in business since 1969, and was even the subject of a reality TV show on *The Playboy Channel*. They are also the only strip club in town that is fully nude and has full alcohol service. Most clubs are one or the other (fully nude and no alcohol, or topless and serving alcohol), but you get both at the Palomino Club. They also have male dancers every Friday, Saturday, and Sunday with shows starting at 10:45 p.m., but get there early to enjoy their happy-hour specials.

OLYMPIC GARDEN
1531 S. Las Vegas Blvd.
702.386.9200
www.ogvegas.com

This is the only strip club on *the Strip* that has both female strippers and a male revue show. The ladies strip downstairs (in a 20,000-square-foot venue) and the men take off their clothes upstairs in a smaller area. The guys are there Sunday, Wednesday, and Thursday from 9 p.m. to 1 a.m., and Friday and Saturday from 8 p.m. to 4 a.m. So it's perfect if you're in town in the middle of the week and want to see some sexy guys. They also have a nice couples package that includes a limousine ride to the club, a bottle of champagne, and a VIP table. If you can't make it to one of the male revue shows, you can catch any of the sexy ladies 24/7.

SHOWGIRL VIDEO
631 S. Las Vegas Blvd.
702.385.4554
www.showgirllive.com

This adult video store north of the Stratosphere is definitely an old-school place. Their exotic sign out front screams retro-Vegas, as do the peep-show booths inside. They have concrete imprints of various body parts from many porn stars on a "Legends of Erotica Walk of Fame." Once inside they offer live nude dancers, who work on tips only, and one-on-one fantasy booths. You'll also find porn videos and sex toys inside to take home with you.

BROTHELS

Contrary to popular belief, prostitution is not legal in the Las Vegas city limits. It's a bit of a drive to get to a brothel, but worth it if you plan right. Driving can take up to forty minutes, so you can hire a taxi, a private limousine or town car with your lover, or a party bus with your girlfriends if you don't feel like making the drive.

Brothels can be a fun place to let loose, even if you're not looking for sex. They have a bar, so you can easily grab a drink, chat with the girls, and be a voyeur. Make sure to tip the ladies for their time even if you're not there for sex. If nothing else, think of it like a scouting mission so you can get comfortable and then come back another day for actual playtime. You can always have your partner watch you and one of the girls if you don't want him to join in, or watch your partner have fun with someone else. You may be surprised at how big of a turn-on it can be. The sky's the limit! If you're planning on going out in Las Vegas at night, it's best to visit in the afternoon as it can take an hour to get to one and then another hour back.

THE CHICKEN RANCH
10511 Homestead Rd., Pahrump
877.585.2397/702.382.7870
www.chickenranchbrothel.com

The Chicken Ranch will pick you up from Las Vegas for free! You can check out the girls on their website and even read their "menu of services" to see what might be right for you. Some of the girls love ladies and couples, and they often feature Penthouse Pets and adult film performers like Sunset Thomas. And there's always something going on at The Chicken Ranch, so visit their website for an updated schedule of naughty events.

SHERI'S RANCH
10551 Homestead Rd., Pahrump
866.820.9100
www.sherisranch.com

Sheri's Ranch is the only Nevada brothel that offers a hotel on property, including a restaurant and sports lounge. So you can treat yourself to a naughty weekend by yourself or with your lover, as you can play 24/7 with any one of the ladies. They even have a volleyball court, pool, and spa. They were awarded "Brothel of the Year" in 2012 and have nice VIP suites (for private parties), which all include their own wet bar, fireplace, and Jacuzzi. Check out their themed bungalows if you're in the mood for a Roman fantasy, a sexy safari, or a swinging 1960s orgy.

THE BUNNY RANCH
69 Moonlight Rd., Carson City
775.246.9901
www.bunnyranch.com

The famous Bunny Ranch has a lot of beautiful girls (including some adult film stars) and some wild stuff on the menu like "The Porn Star Experience," "Tantric Sex," "Three Girl Party," and "Sybian Experience." Make sure to check out their other brothels: LoveRanch North, LoveRanch Southern NV and Alien Cathouse where you can live out your alien fantasies.

MUSTANG RANCH
1000 Wild Horse Canyon Dr., Sparks
800.727.8638
www.mustangranchbrothel.com

The Mustang Ranch has a full bar, an ATM on site, and they accommodate all budgets. They're the furthest from Las Vegas (at least an eight-hour drive), but if you're taking a road trip to Reno or on your way home, this is an ideal stop. For those who might not be looking for sex (but just a tease), they offer a full menu of services such as their striptease, vibrator, girl-on-girl, and shower shows. Or maybe you want a little foreplay? Then you can choose from their nude massage, breast massage, or bubble bath—to name a few. Or if you want to go all the way, then you'll want to pick off of their "Full Pleasure" menu.

MALE & FEMALE ESCORTS

If you want to hire a female escort in Las Vegas, don' worry. It's easy as pie. There are so many opportunities to hire female escorts that it would be impossible to list them all. But if you don't want to take your chances on a number from a random flyer handed to you by someone on the Vegas sidewalks, then you'll find some valid and professional options on the next pages. Hiring an escort for the evening can be a great gift idea for you and your lover, for a night on the town and maybe even back to your room for a magical evening.

Finding a male escort is trickier. Most internet ads are for gay men, but you can find straight guys who will not only look good on your arm as you walk into a nightclub, but also look good wearing a bath towel or less. It's a great idea to hire an escort for a date if you're coming to Vegas solo or with your lover—you may even want to hire a male and a female escort for double the pleasure! Escorts provide anything from a night on the town, massage, or just someone to talk with over drinks. If things go well, you might end up with a date you'll remember the rest of your life.

LARUE MCCAY

www.laruemccay.com

LaRue McCay is a successful pinup, fashion model, fire performer and professional companion all rolled up into one, gorgeous, sexy and dynamic package. With her classic dark-haired, fair-skinned good looks and an intelligent and agile mind, LaRue is everything you could want in a companion for a night out in Sin City. She is respectful, professional and encourages couples to join her for a special night where you're encouraged to reimagine yourself as a couple, explore new territories and reclaim the intimacy of your romance. LaRue is an elite escort based in Las Vegas, but she is able to travel if a travel partner is what you're searching for. Check out her website for more information.

COWBOYS 4 ANGELS

www.cowboys4angels.com

This service has some really hot guys who specialize in treating you like you're the only woman in the world. Some of their "cowboys" are featured on the reality show *Gigolos*. They provide safe, attractive gentleman who offer more than just physical intimacy. They can be a pleasant date, eye candy at a big event you're attending, or even share a drink with you while you're a stranger in town.

TAWNY BRIE
www.tawnybrie.com

Tawny Brie is a beautiful, sexy and delightful companion available for single dates or for couples who are interested in spicing up their love life. Tawny receives much pleasure out of helping couples rekindle that sexual spark and intimacy. Versatile, intelligent, stimulating and bold, this strawberry blonde bombshell is full of surprises and twists and turns. Clean and professional, Tawny makes for a great girlfriend date on the town or she can excel as a companion in the naughty world of Vegas Strip Clubs and Swingers Events. Tawny is comfortable in all worlds! Check out her website and see if you want to experience the night of your life!

MEET SARAH BLAKE
www.meetsarahblake.com

Sarah Blake is a talented model/actress hailing from America's Heartland. With her relaxed demeanor, easy-going charm and warmth, Sarah makes the perfect companion, just for the evening or for longer periods of time. She enjoys spending time with others and sharing in their fantasies and desires, while also staying busy as a producer of fetish videos, dancing and acting in films. Sarah is a professional, engaging and courteous companion who believes in discretion and privacy and a night with her is one that you will not soon forget. Women are encouraged to contact her as well, so don't be shy!

ABOUT THE AUTHOR

NAUGHTY LIFESTYLE EXPERT
WWW.NAUGHTYLIFESTYLEEXPERT.COM

Sienna Sinclaire moved to Los Angeles in December 2006, after living in London, UK, where she used to work for a magazine. She quickly fell in love with L.A. and its naughty side. And with Vegas being so close, Sienna became a regular visitor. These naughty pilgrimages inspired her to write her second book, "Naughty Girl's Guide to Las Vegas." She currently resides in Santa Monica, CA, where she's a writer, sex coach, model, and Naughty Lifestyle Expert.

ABOUT THE PHOTOGRAPHER

ARCHERSTEVENS@GMAIL.COM

Archer Stevens has been shooting amazing locations, beautiful people, and naughty girls for twenty-seven years. He's known for his mastery of natural lighting in outdoor settings. He helps to bring out women's natural beauty in all his shoots. Born and raised in Northern California, Archer currently resides in Portland, OR, but travels all over the U.S. If you'd like to book him for a photo shoot you can email him at the above address.

BIBLIOGRAPHY

Ferrari, Michelle and Stephen Ives. *Las Vegas An Unconventional History*. New York: Bulfinch Press, 2005.

Land, Barbara and Myrick Land. *A Short History of Las Vegas*. Reno: University of Nevada Press, 2004.

Las Vegas: An Unconventional History. Dir. Stephen Ives. PBS, 2005. Film.

Sheehan, Jack. *Skin City: Uncovering the Las Vegas Sex Industry*. Stephens Press, 2004.

The Real Las Vegas. Dir. Jim Milio and Melissa Jo Peltier. The History Channel, 2001. Film.

Vegas The City The Mob Made. Dir. Ron Meyer. Mill Creek Entertainment, 2009. Film.

Works Cited

1. Kishi, Stephanie. Home of Sin City's Original Sin. May 15. 2008. Retrieved from http://www.lasvegassun.com/news/2008/may/15/origination-sin-sin-city/

2. History. (n.d.). para. 2. Retrieved from http://www.elkshelldorado.com/history

3. History - The 1990s: King Arthur Meets King Tut. (n.d.). para. 1. Retrieved from http://www.frommers.com/destinations/las-vegas/685671

Website Sources

Larker, Amy. *Gentlemen's Clubs and Casinos in Las Vegas.* UNLV. http://digitalscholarship.unlv.edu/

DenverGambler. *Turning Back the Clock: El Rancho Vegas.* Vegas Chatter. http://www.vegaschatter.com/story/2012/5/16/16253/8949/vegas-travel/Turning+Back+the+Clock%3A+El+Rancho+Vegas. 2012

History. Elks Helldorado. http://www.elkshelldorado.com/history

Palomino Strip Club. Vegas Total Access.http://www.vegastotalaccess.com/StripClubs/Palomino.html. 2008

Finnegan, Amanda. *Resorts Weigh Pros and Cons of Topless Pool Scene.* Las Vegas Sun. http://www.lasvegassun.com/news/2010/may/11/are-parties-worth-trouble/. 2010

Las Vegas Returns to Sin City Roots. ABC News. http://abcnews.go.com/2020/story? id=132628

Shulman, Michael and Susan Michals. *The New Burlesque of Las Vegas.* Vegas Magazine. http://vegasmagazine.com/personalities/articles/the-new-burlesque

The Dunes Hotel History - The Miracle in the Desert - 1960s. Classic Las Vegas. http://classiclasvegas.squarespace.com/a-brief-history-of-the-strip/?currentPage=25. 2008

Dusty Summers. Burlesque Hall of Fame. http://www.burlesquehall.com/dustysummers/. 2011

Lido at the Stardust. UNLV. http://digital.library.unlv.edu/collections/showgirls/lidostardust

Timeline: Las Vegas. PBS. http://www.pbs.org/wgbh/amex/lasvegas/timeline/. 2005

History. City of Las Vegas. http://www.lasvegasnevada.gov/factsstatistics/history.htm

Welcome to Divorce Nevada Style. Divorce Seekers. http://divorceseekers.wordpress.com/2012/07/10/welcome-to-divorce-nevada-style/. 2012

A Brief History of Las Vegas. Sunset Cities. http://www.sunsetcities.com/lasvegas/lasvegashistory.html

How Las Vegas Got Into the Nevada Divorce Business. Divorce Seekers. http://divorceseekers.wordpress.com/2013/06/16/nevada-as-a-place-to-split-is-a-legend-of-ourtime/.2013

Femme Fatale: Lili St Cyr. Java's Bachelor Pad. http://javasbachelorpad.com/cyr.html

La Rouge, Femme Vivre. *Burlesque Arrests: Lili St Cyr.* Pin Curl Magazine. http://pincurlmag.com/burlesque-arrests-lili-st-cyr. 2011

Lili St Cyr. Wikipedia. http://en.wikipedia.org/wiki/Lili_St._Cyr

Lili St Cyr Biography. IMDb. http://www.imdb.com/name/nm0820506/bio

Burlesque History VII: Lili St Cyr. Dollhouse Bettie. http://www.dollhousebettie.com/index.php?option=com_myblog&Itemid=0&lang=en&show=399

The Hotel Last Frontier History. Classic Las Vegas. http://classiclasvegas.squarespace.com/a-brief-history-of-the-strip/2007/7/6/the-hotel-lastfrontier-history.html. 2007

Frontier Village & The Silver Slipper. In Old Las Vegas. http://www.inoldlasvegas.com/silver_slipper.html

Taylor, Andrew F. *Red Light Lectures Share Valle's Colorful Prostitution History.* Review Journal. http://www.reviewjournal.com/life/community-organizations/red-light-lectures-sharevalleys-colorful-prostitution-history. 2012

Prostitution in Nevada. Wikipedia. http://en.wikipedia.org/wiki/Prostitution_in_Nevada

L, Jeremy. *Nevada Brothel History (Past and Present).* Sheri's Ranch. http://www.sherisranch.com/nevada-brothels/

The Entertainers. PBS. http://www.pbs.org/wgbh/amex/lasvegas/peopleevents/p_entertainers.html. 2005

Sex and Lies in Las Vegas - Page 2. The Roaming Gambler. http://www.theroaminggambler.com/site/redlight2.html

Kishi, Stephanie. *Home of Sin City's Original Sin.* Las Vegas Sun. http://www.lasvegassun.com/news/2008/may/15/origination-sin-sin-city/. 2008

Comella, Lynn. *Looking at the History of Prostitution in Las Vegas.* Las Vegas Weekly. http://www.lasvegasweekly.com/news/2012/jul/04/marie-rowley-explores-historyprostitution-las-veg/. 2012

Showgirls. Vegas Retro. http://www.vegasretro.com/glamour/showgirls.html

Burlesque Stars. Vegas Retro. http://www.vegasretro.com/burlesque/burlesque.html

Silver Slipper. Vegas Live Show. http://www.vegasliveshow.com/stage/show-tickets/lasvegas-shows/entertainment/silver-slipper/581

INDEX

PHOTO CREDITS

All photos in the book were taken by Archer Stevens except for the following:

Photos courtesy of:

- Burlesque Hall of Fame: 28
- Caesars Palace: 4-5, 14, 32-33, 46, 52, 57, 78, 84, 86-87, 91, 150, 162-163, 170, 174-175, 191, 208, 222, 225, 227, 233, 240, 244-245, 247, 248, 256-258, 262-263, 266-267, 270, 273-274
- Cowboys 4 Angels: 290
- Erotic Heritage Museum: 200
- La Marie Portraiture: 116, 119
- Las Vegas Acro Entertainment Production: 144-145
- Llyod Rosen Photography: 48, 51, 64, 110, 147, 152-153, 178, 193, 294
- Night School For Girls: 122
- Sapphire: 157
- Skin City: 136, 138
- The Green Door: 212, 216-217
- Thunder From Down Under: 261
- Trapeze Las Vegas: 128

SPECIAL THANKS
to the following people for making this book possible:

Alec Hsu

Archer Stevens

Burlesque Hall of Fame

Caesar's Entertainment

Cowboys 4 Angels

David Barry

Ellen Waugh

Erotic Heritage Museum

Garrett Tomlin

La Marie Portraiture

Las Vegas Acro Entertainment Production

Liza Dodson

Night School For Girls

Nik Havert

Sapphire Gentlemen's Club

Skin City

The Green Door

Thunder From Down Under

Trapeze Las Vegas